#295

3

DELTAFORM PUBLICATIONS LTD.

ISBN 0-9694355-0-9

Published by Deltaform Publications Ltd.
Calgary, Alberta

Printed and Bound in Canada

To Janet

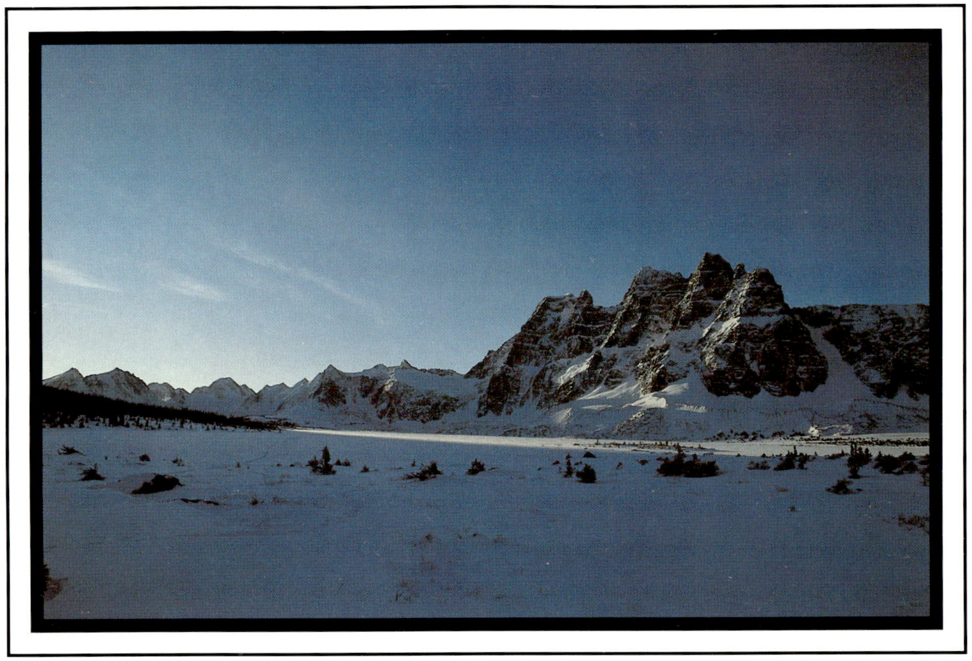

PREFACE

The selection of photographs in this book reflect my personal appreciation for the images that I have found interesting as both an artist and as a mountaineer. Although all of the photographs were taken in the Canadian Rockies, this project was not an attempt to document this area. My intention was to try and capture the movement of light and moments of transition that can make the mountains and their environment so mysterious. It has been my goal to become part of that environment and to capture on film the emotion that the mountain world evokes. I hope that as an artist I have been able to convey these feelings through my work and to generate a sense of respect for these special places.

Anthony Neilson
1990

ANTHONY NEILSON

MOMENTS OF TRANSITION

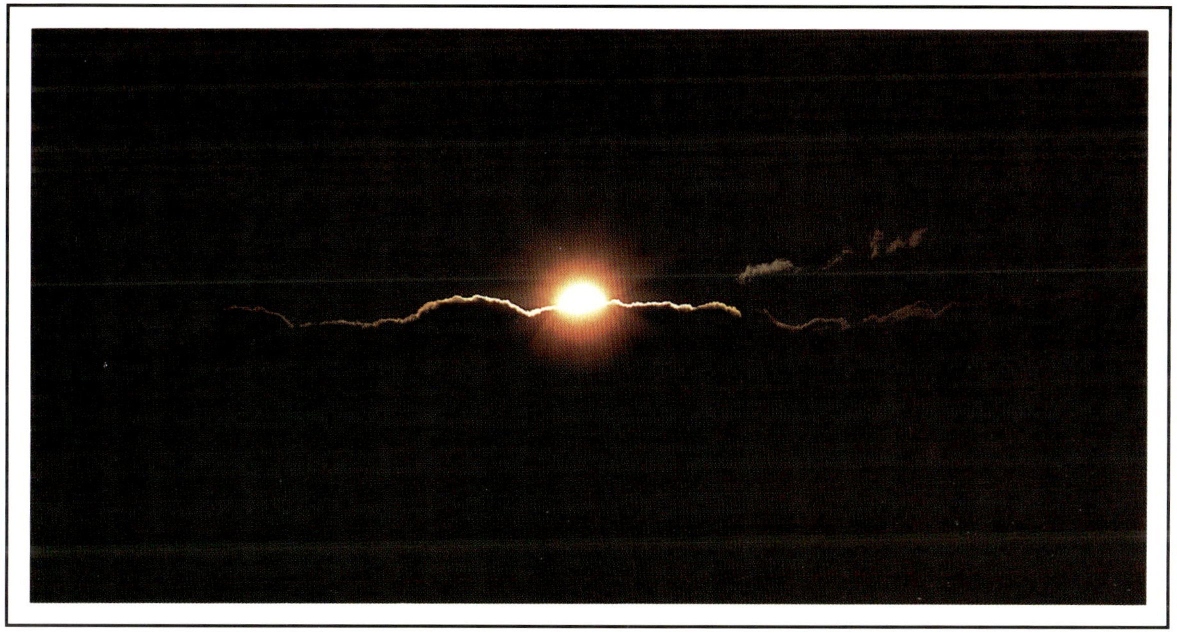

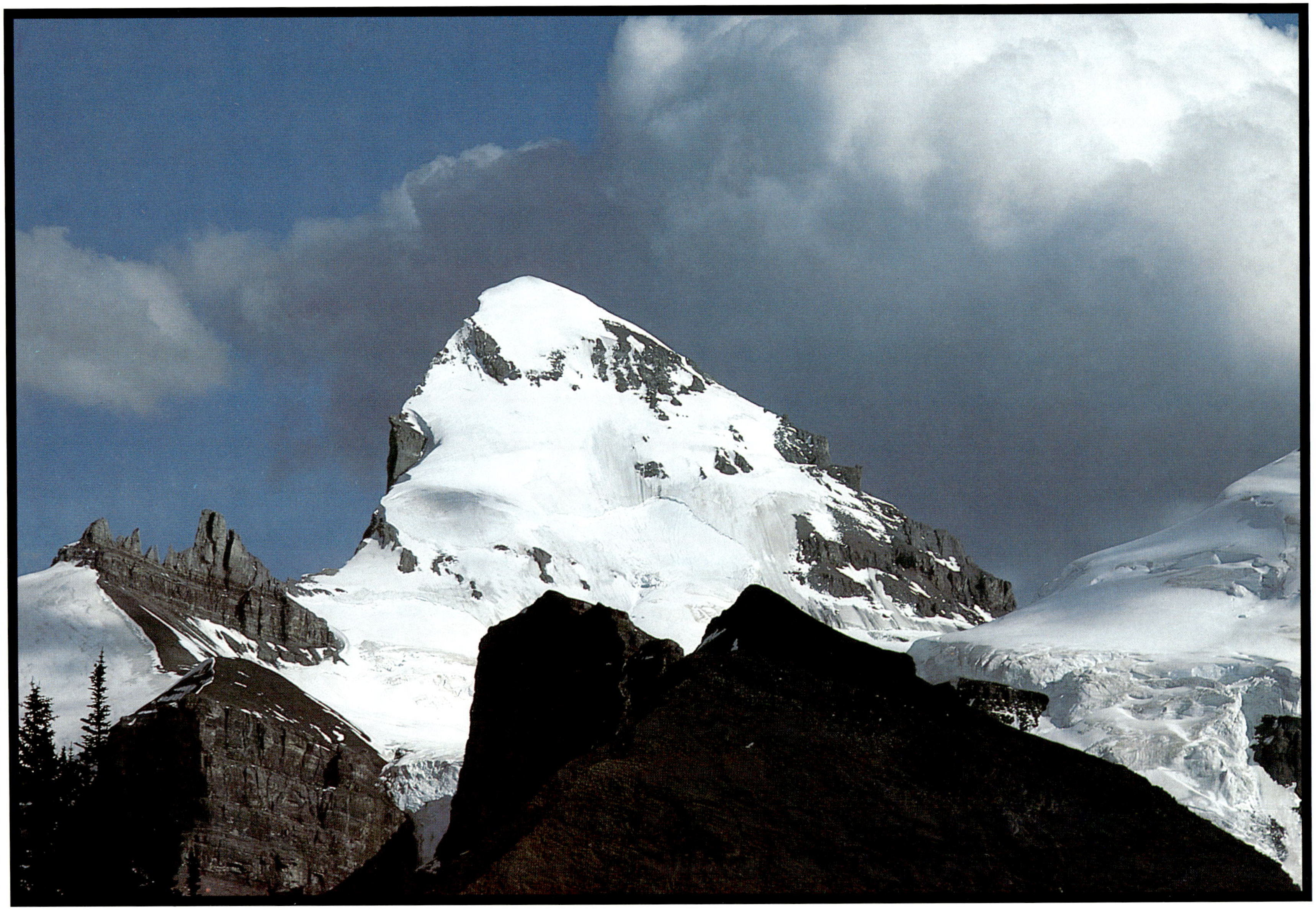

IMAGE #1 MOUNT FORBES

IMAGE #2 MOUNT BRYCE

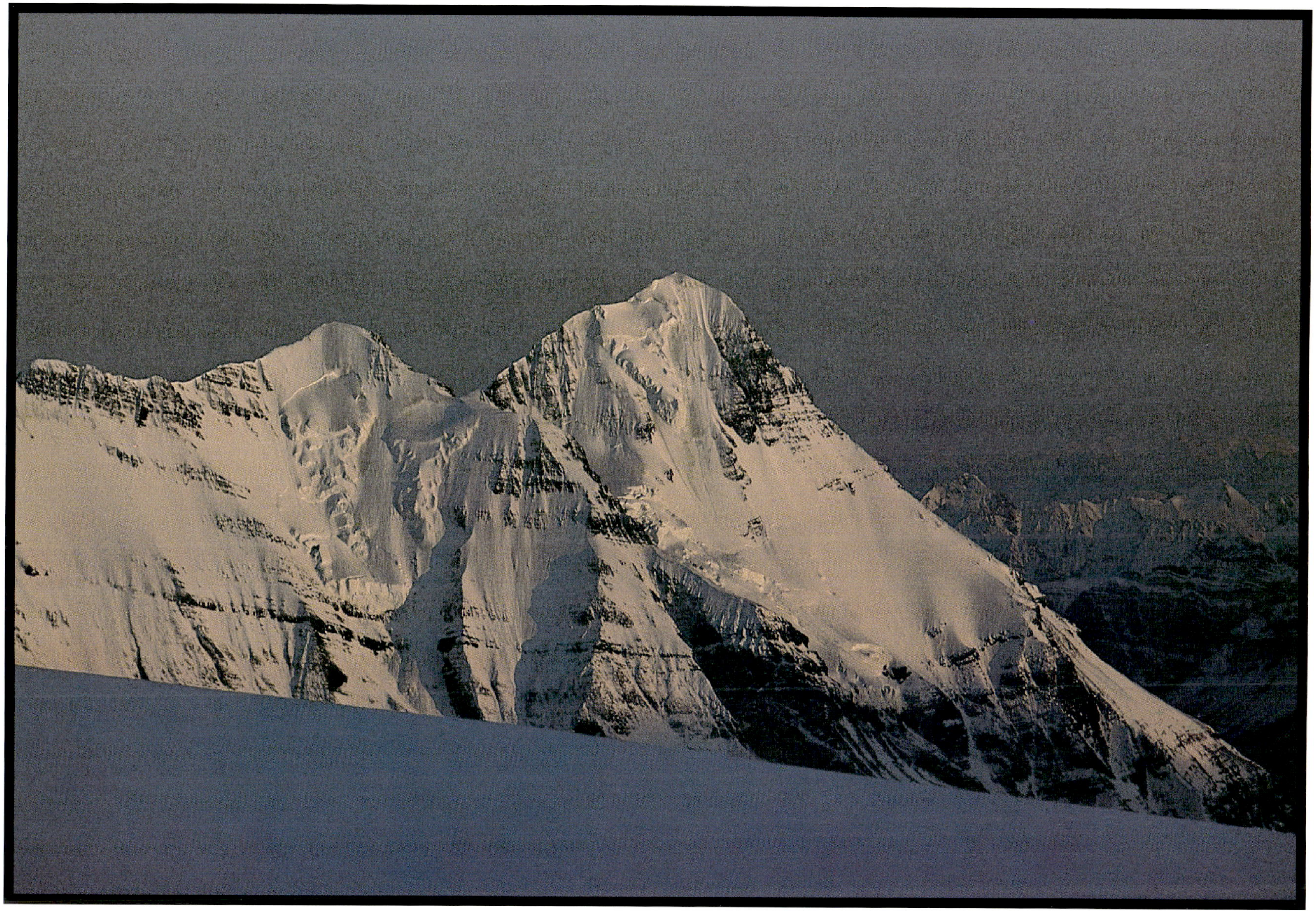

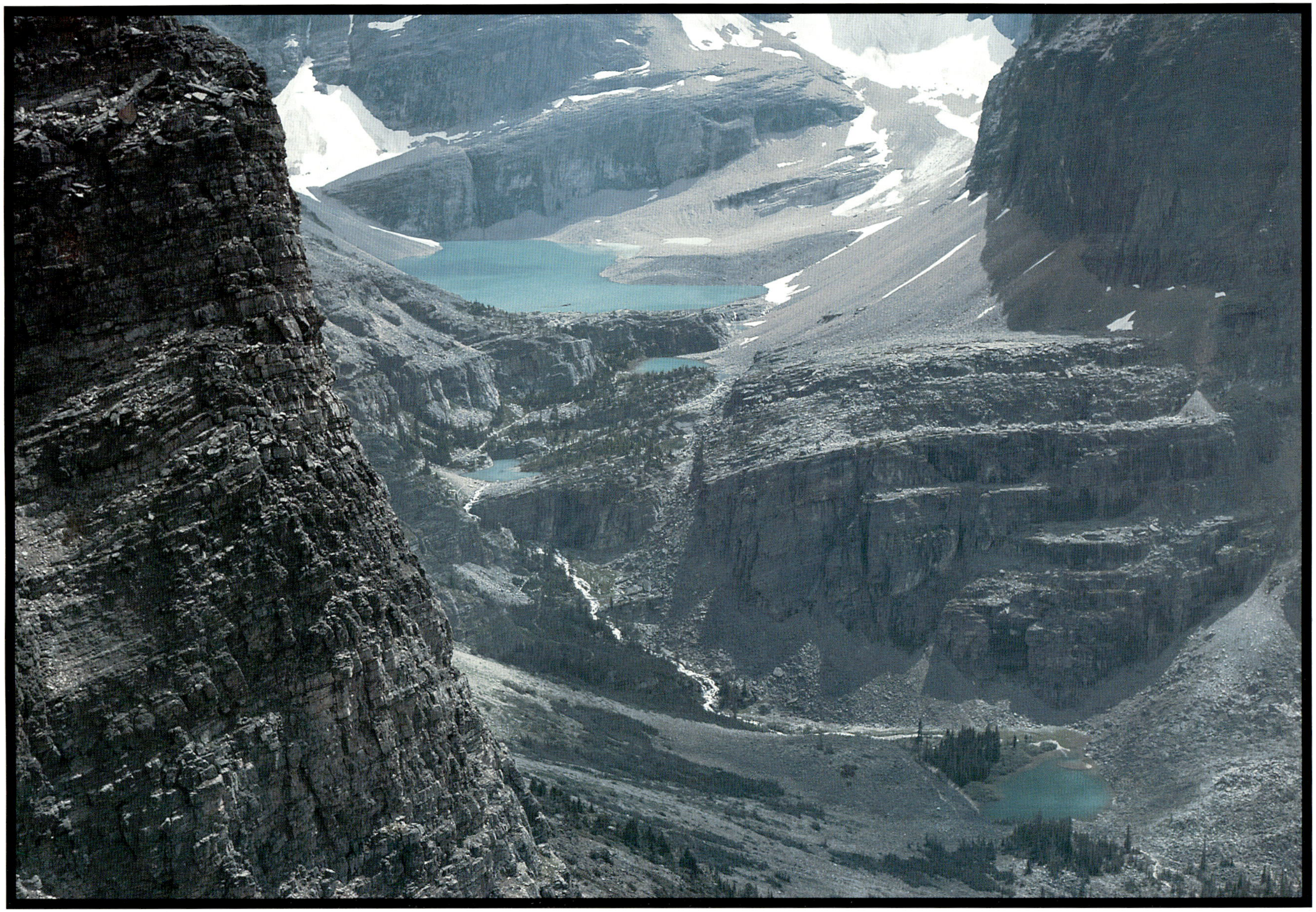

IMAGE #3 LAKE OESA

IMAGE #4 GERALDINE LAKE

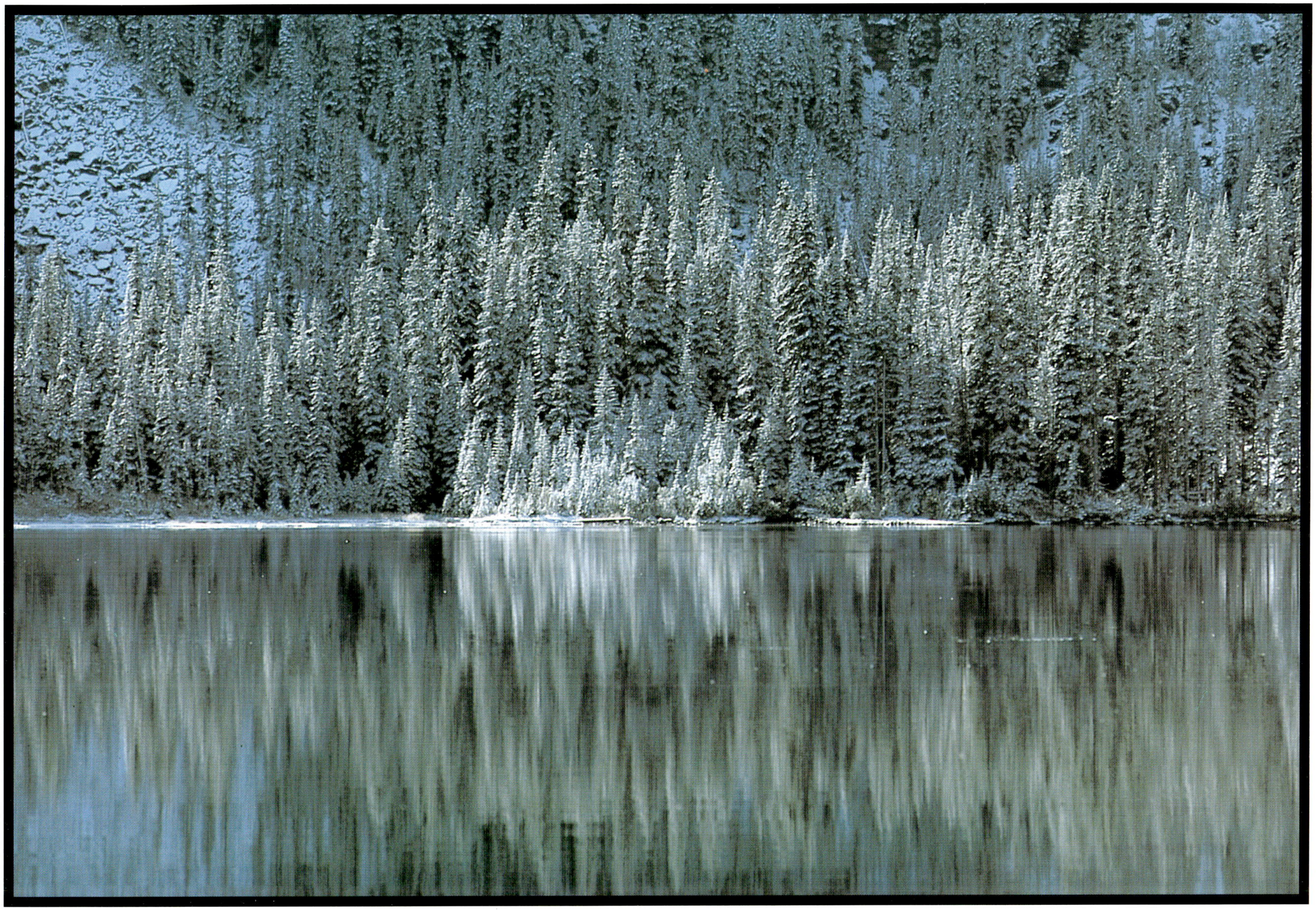

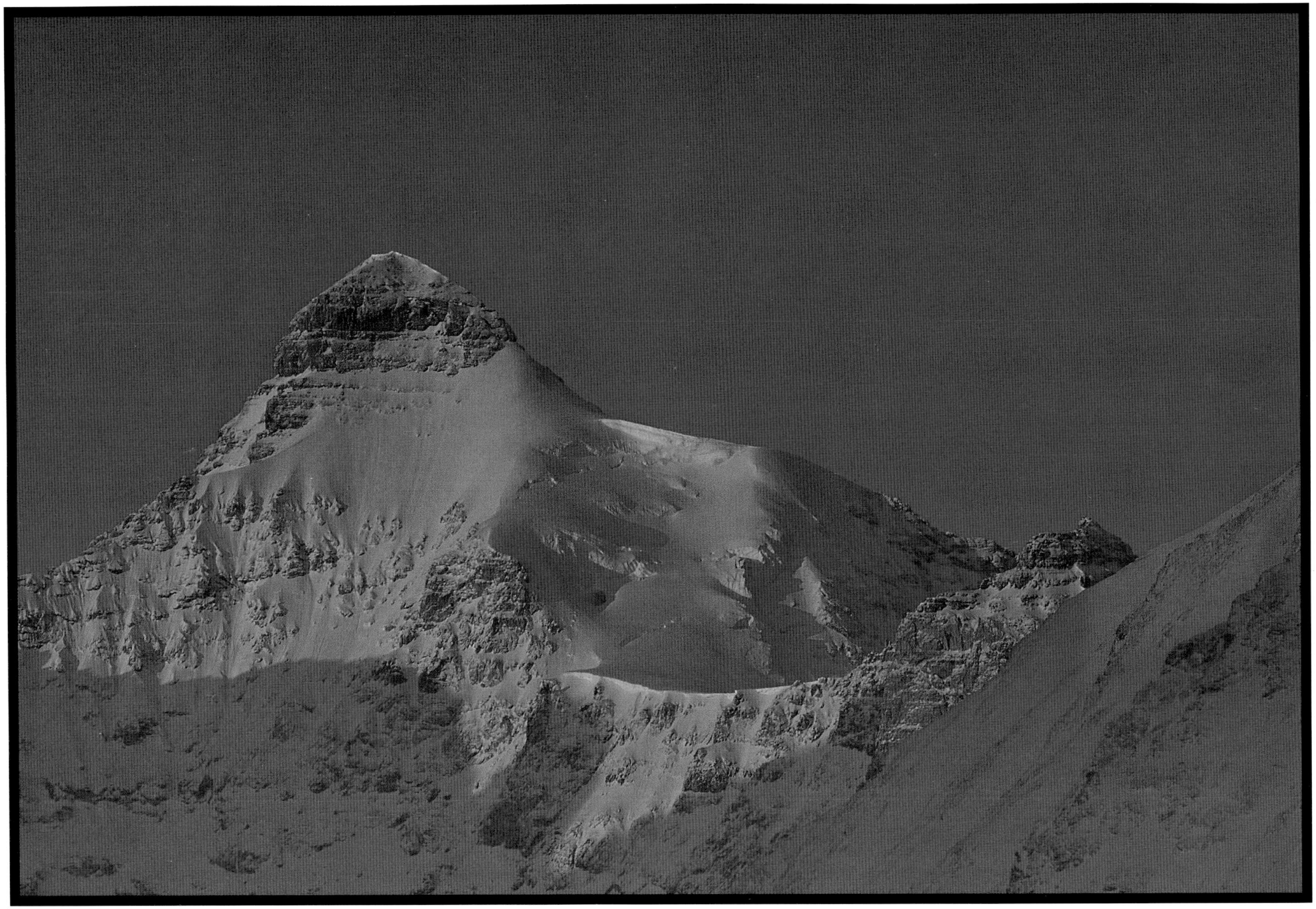

IMAGE #5 MOUNT ATHABASCA

IMAGE #6 GLACIER LAKE

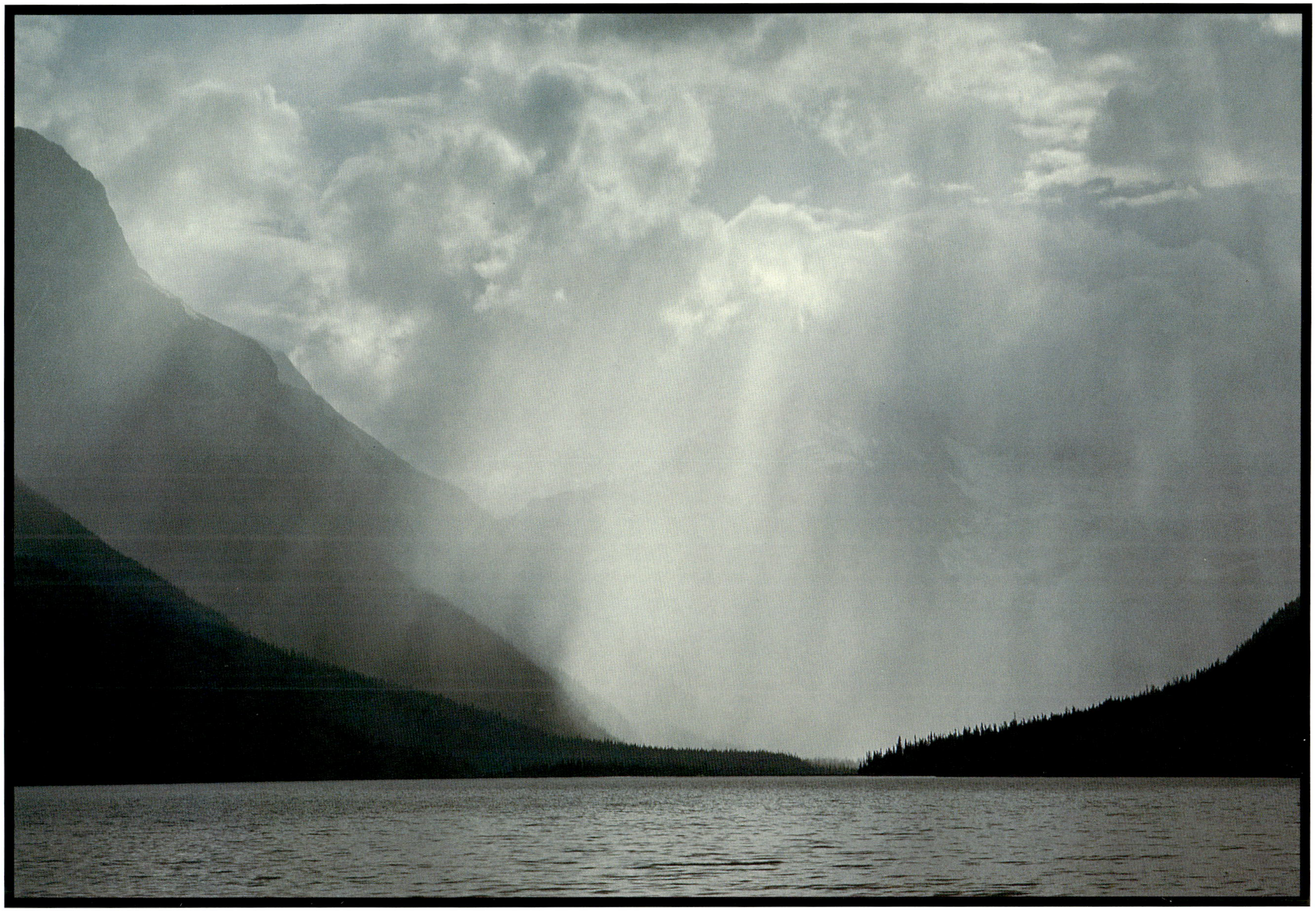

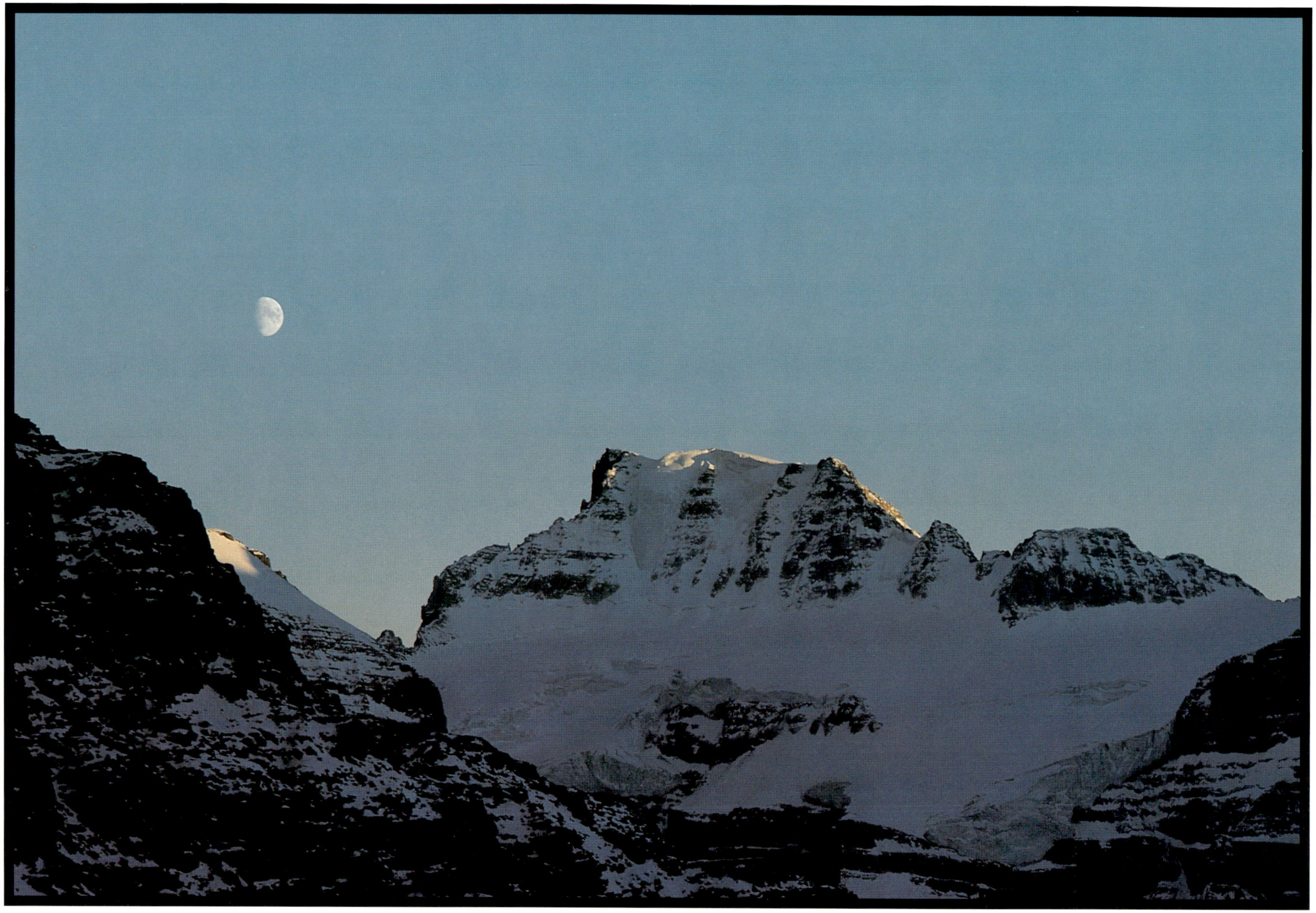

IMAGE #7 MOUNT FAY, MOONRISE

IMAGE #8 MOUNT ROBSON

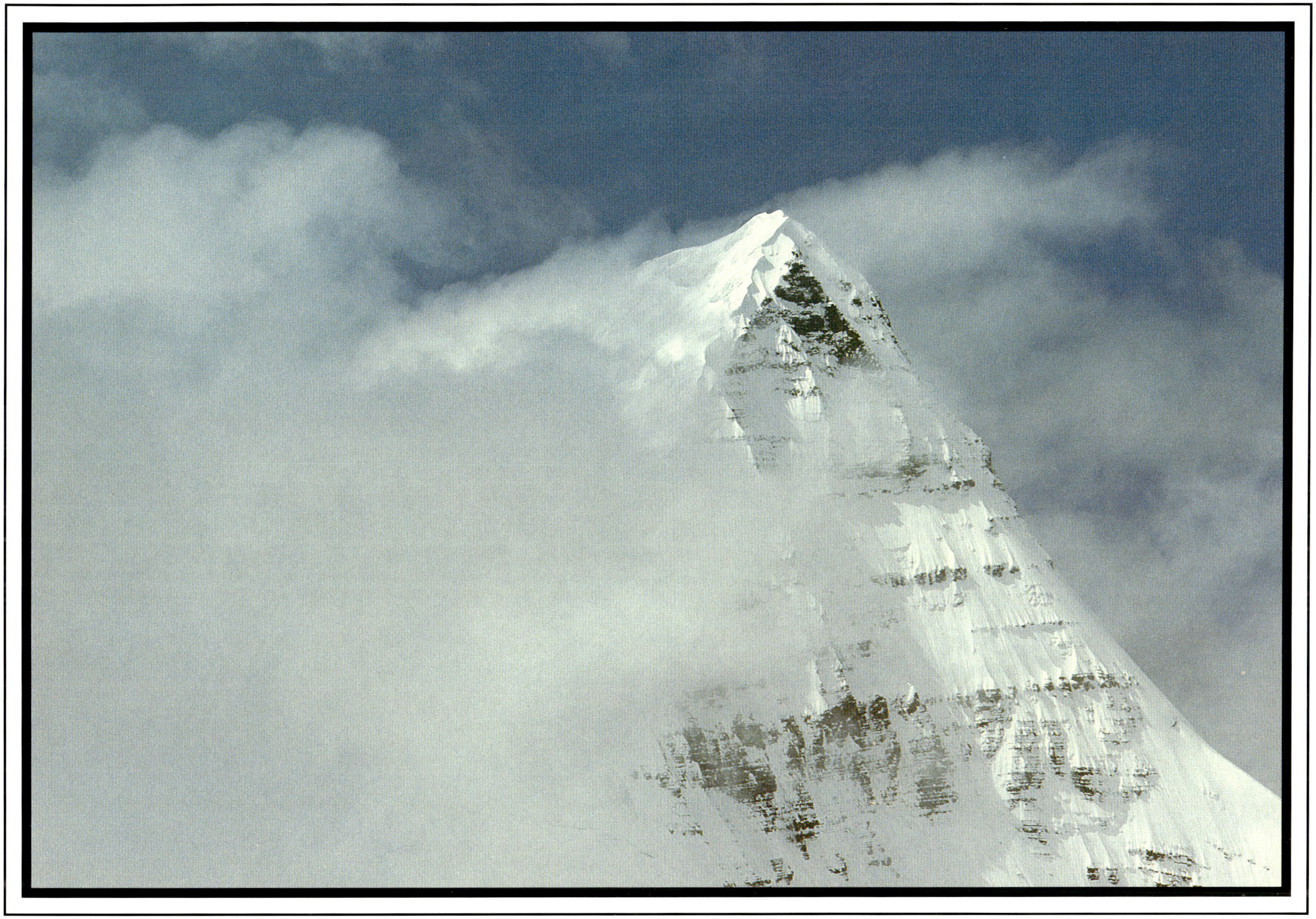

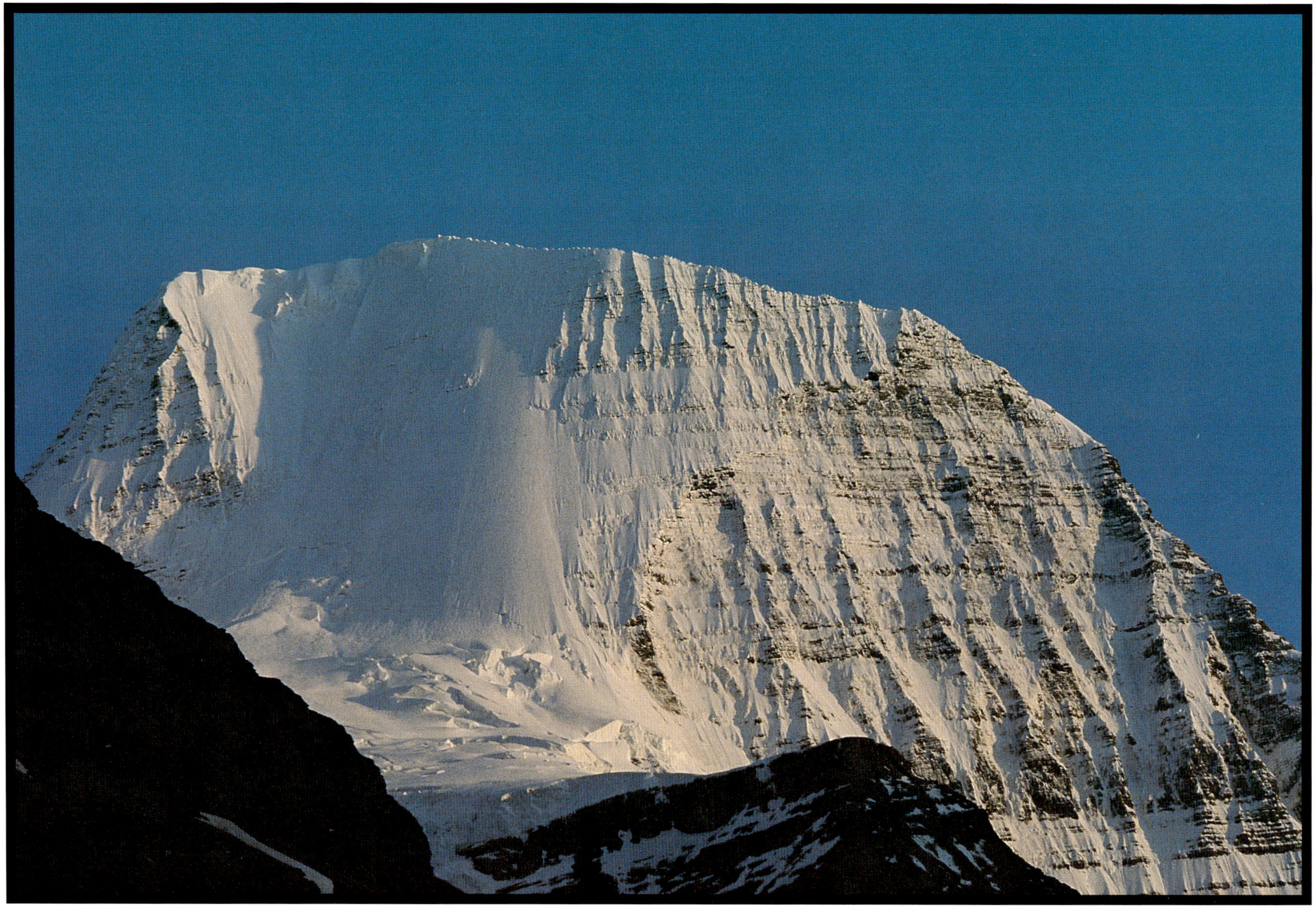

IMAGE #9 MOUNT ROBSON, SUNSET

IMAGE #10 MOUNT ROBSON, MOONRISE

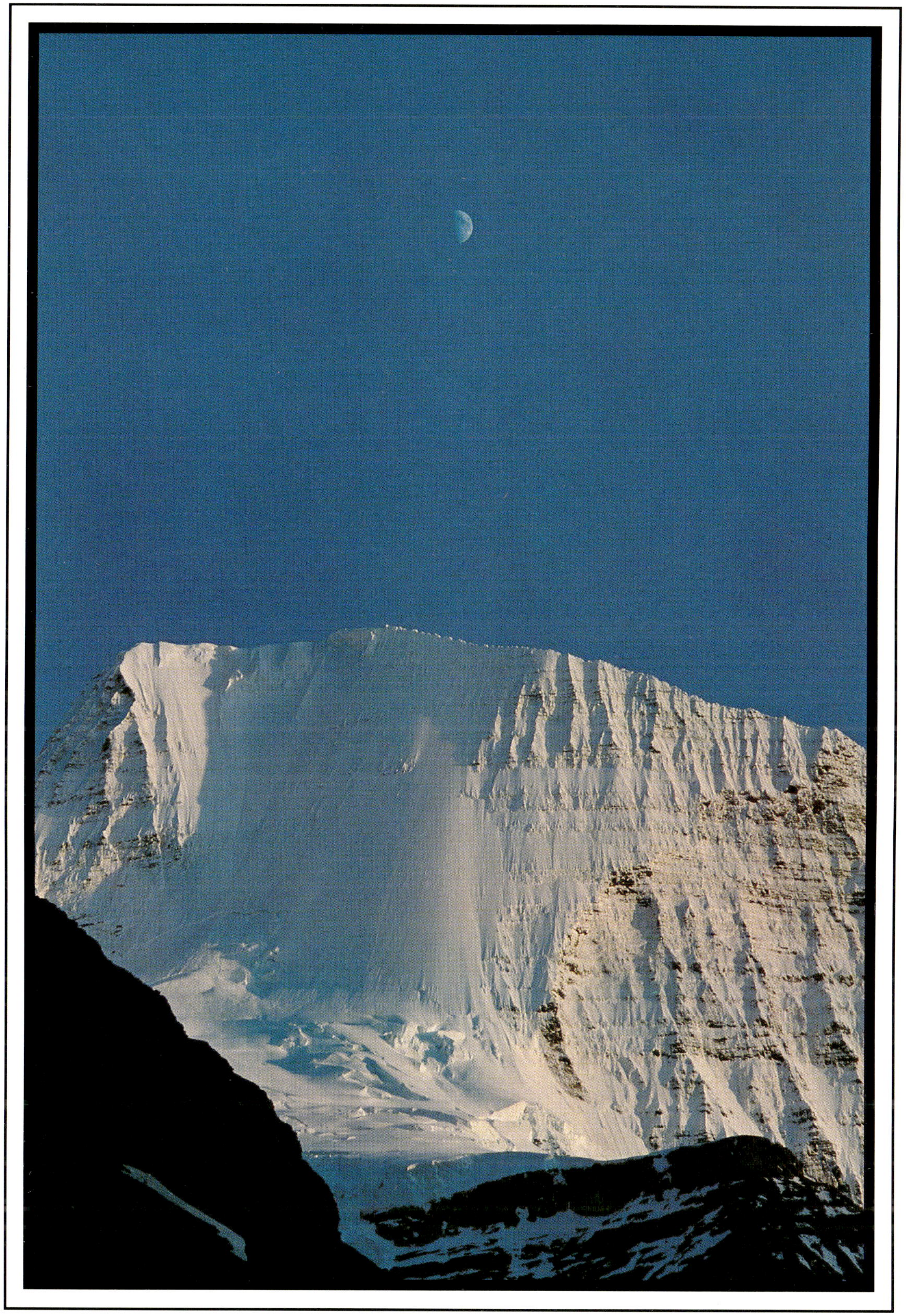

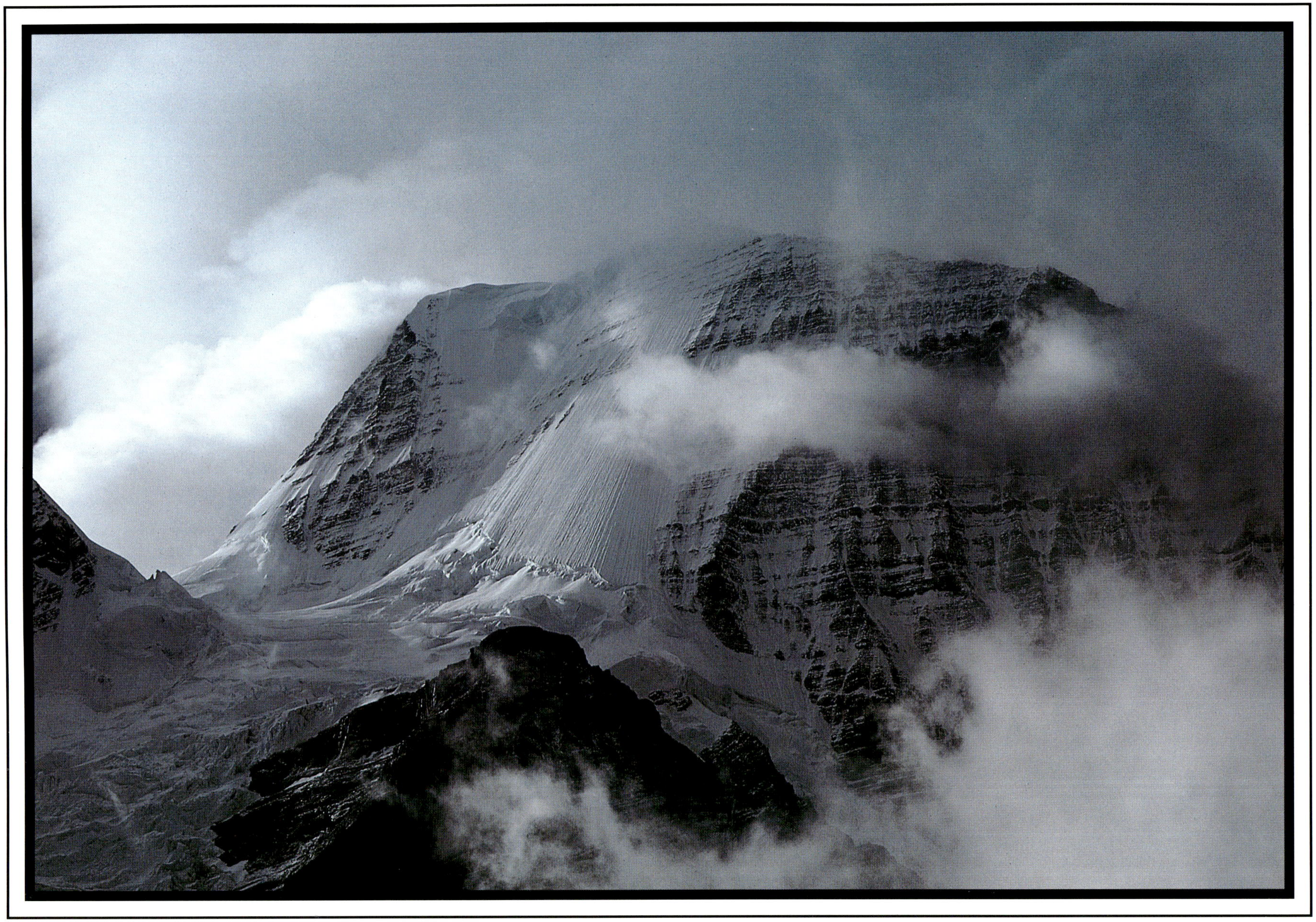

IMAGE #11 MOUNT ROBSON

IMAGE #12 SUNSET AND STORM

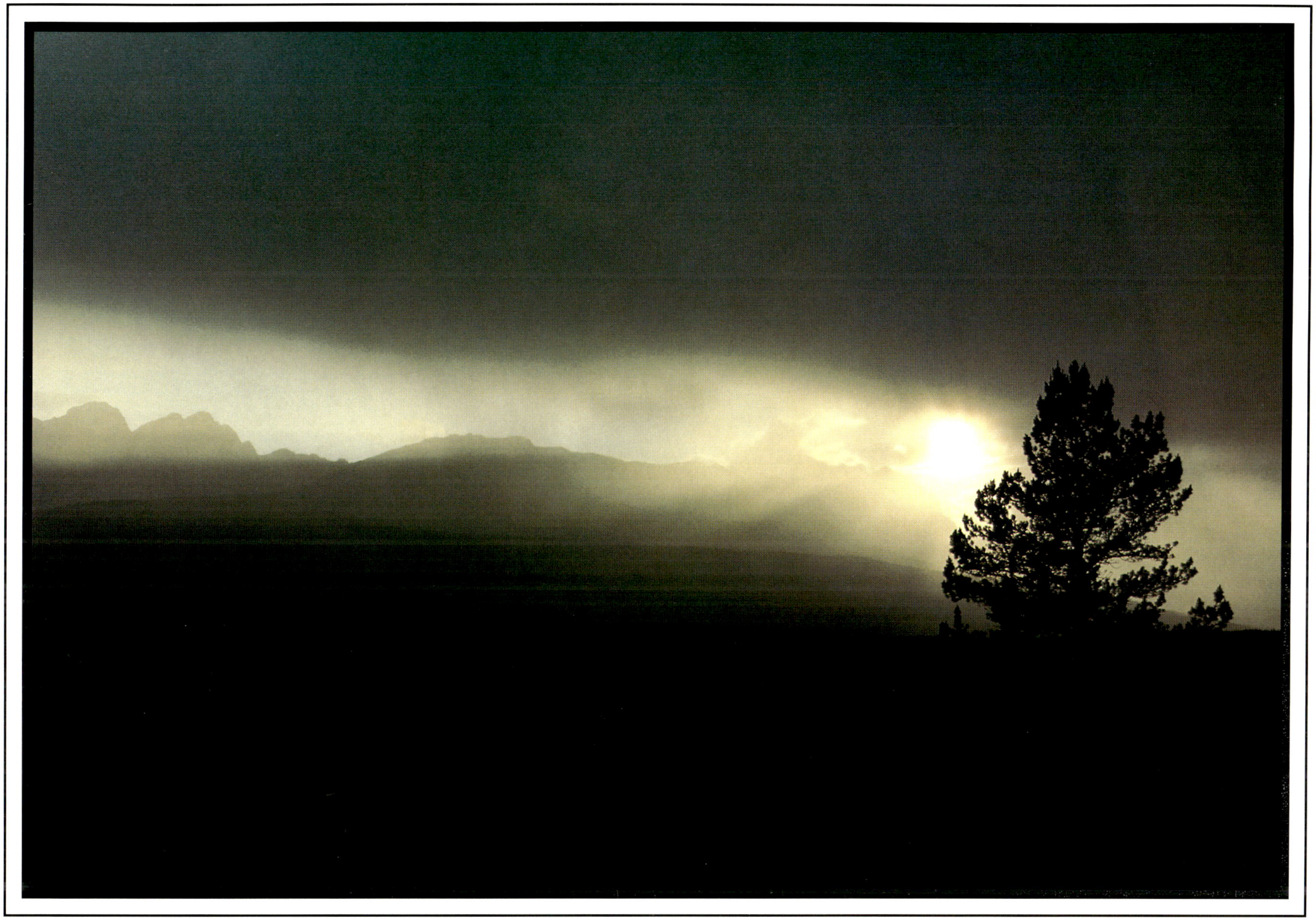

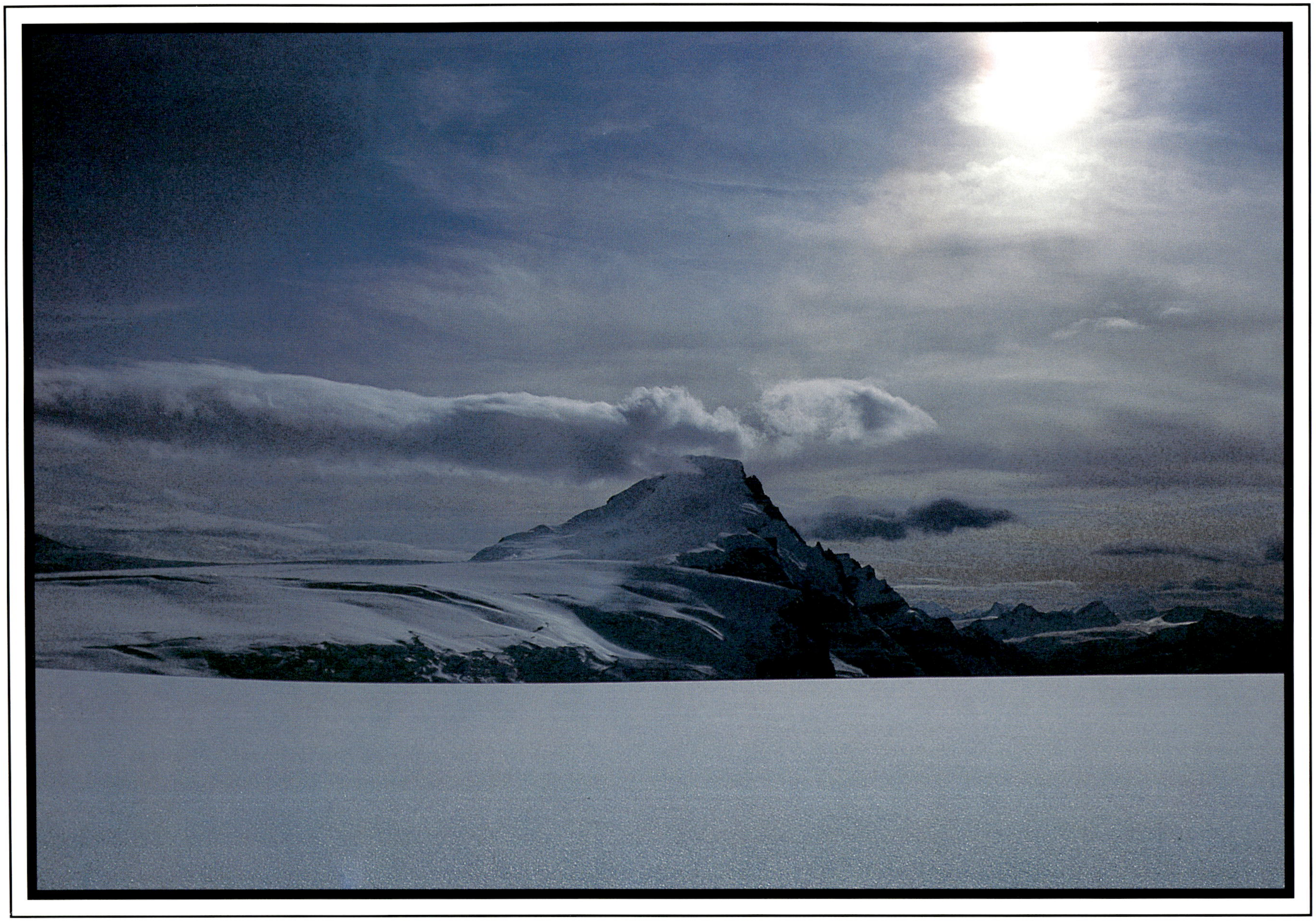

IMAGE #13 MOUNT COLUMBIA

IMAGE #14 MOUNT COLUMBIA, NORTH FACE

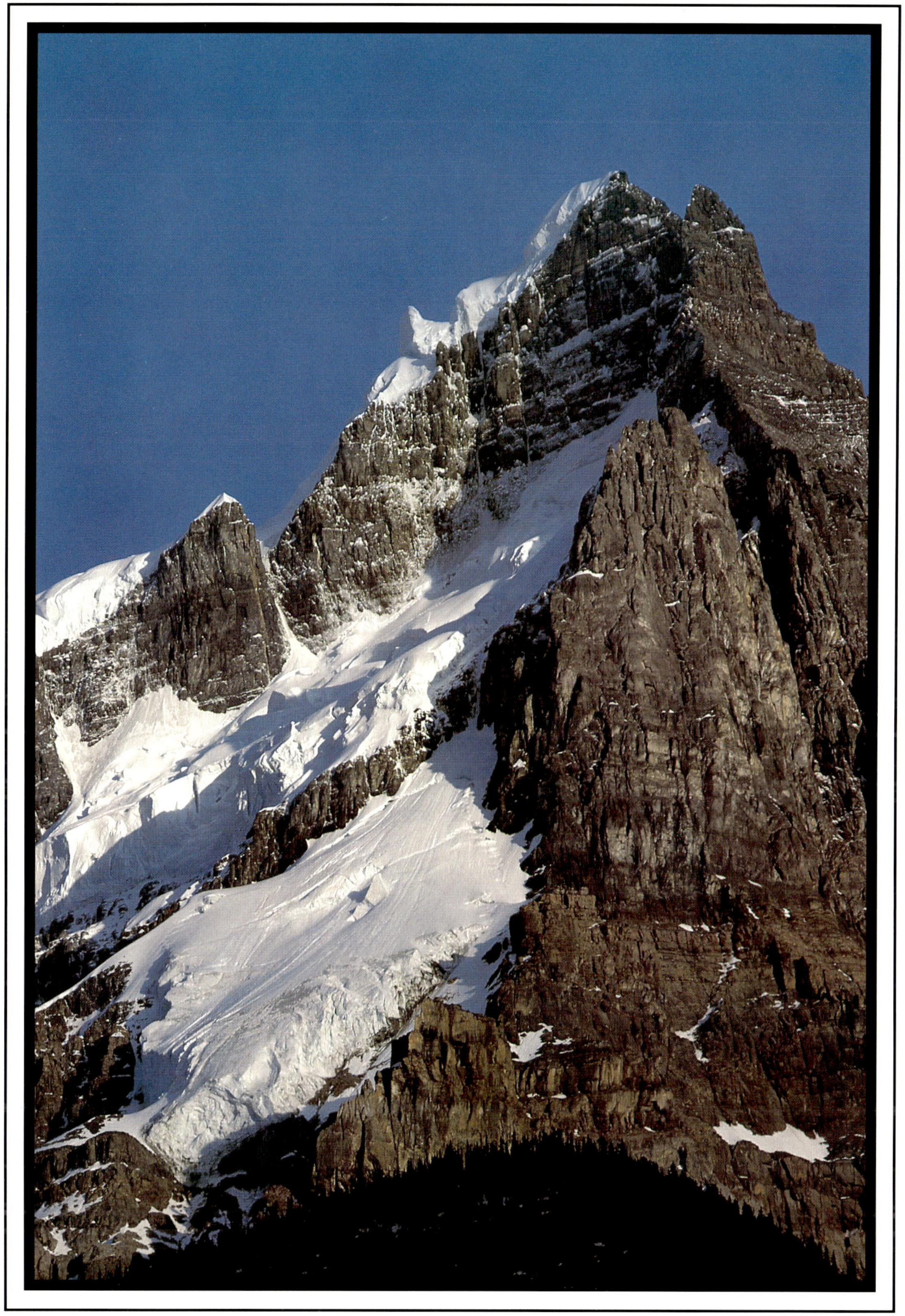

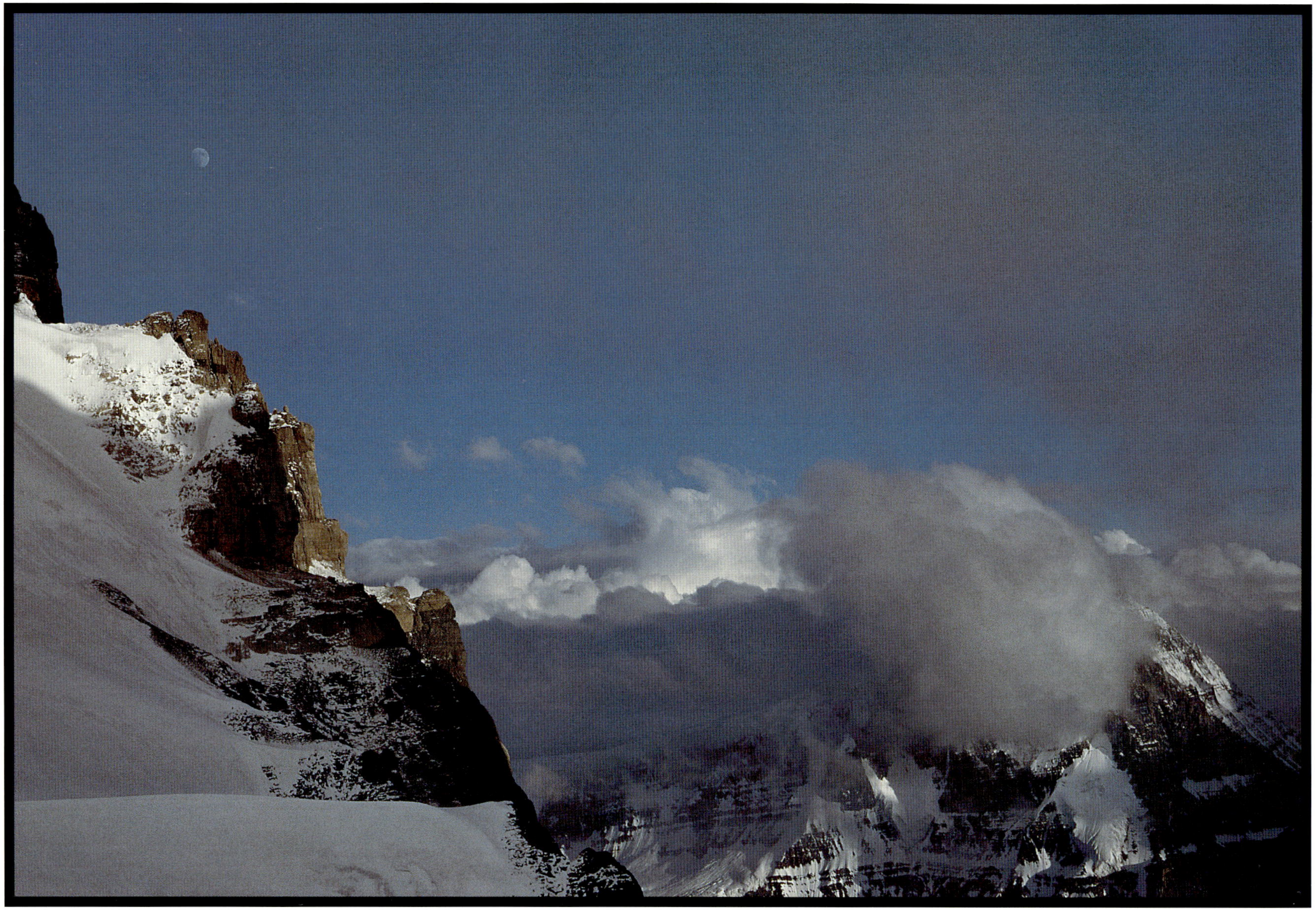

IMAGE #15 MOUNT COLUMBIA, MOONRISE

IMAGE #16 SUNSET FROM MOUNT ASSINABOINE

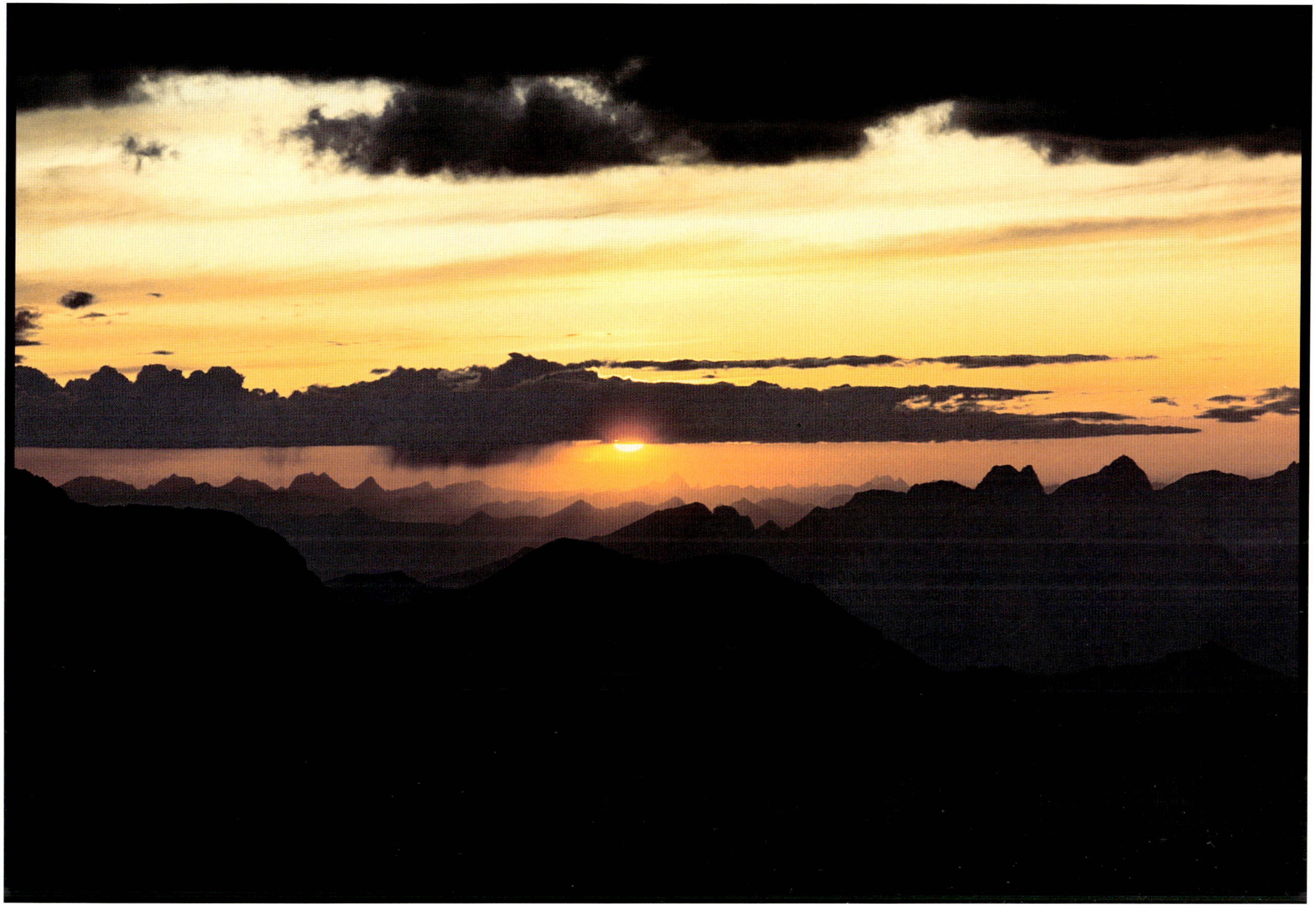

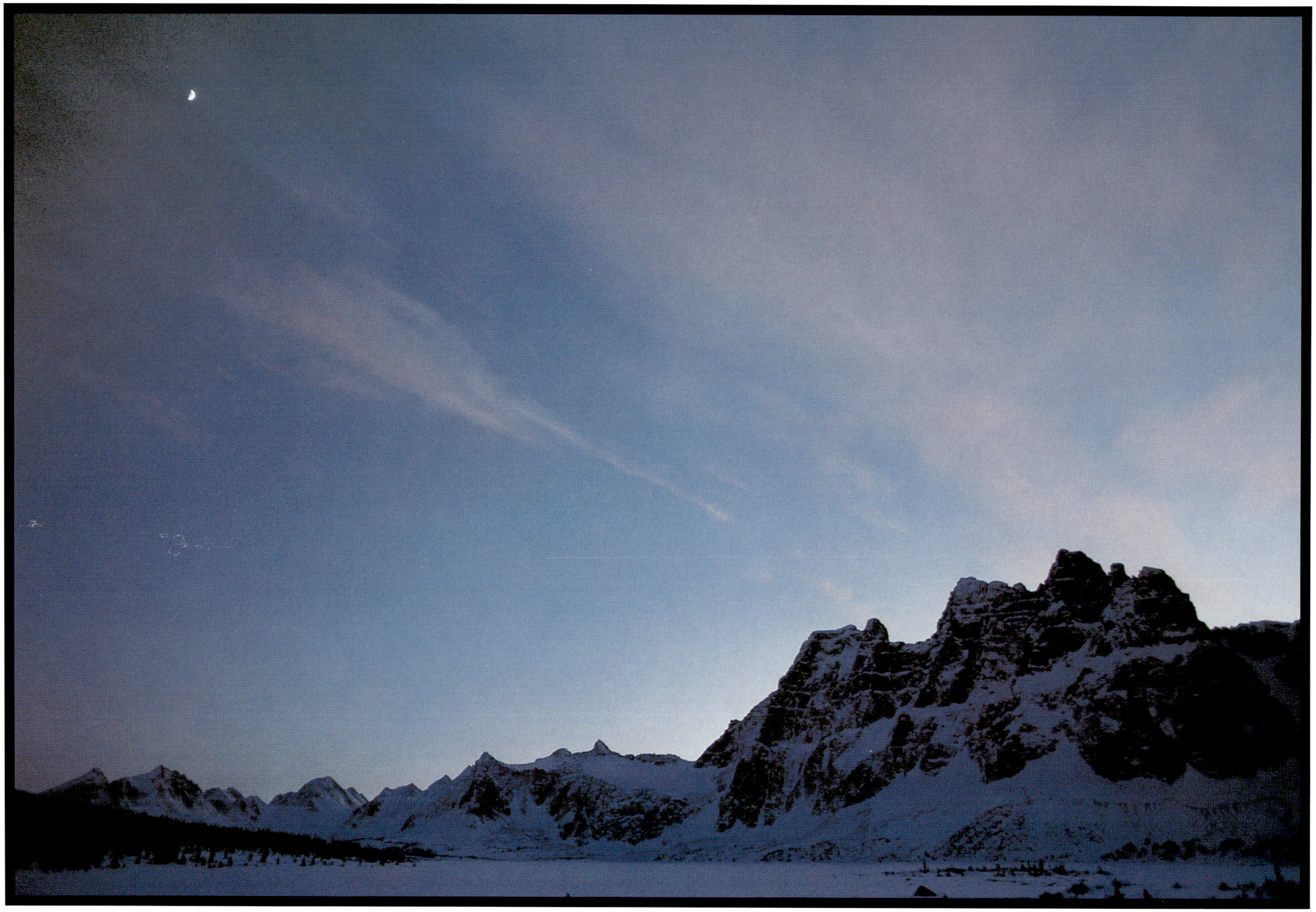

IMAGE #17 THE RAMPARTS, MOONRISE

IMAGE #18 AMETHYST LAKES

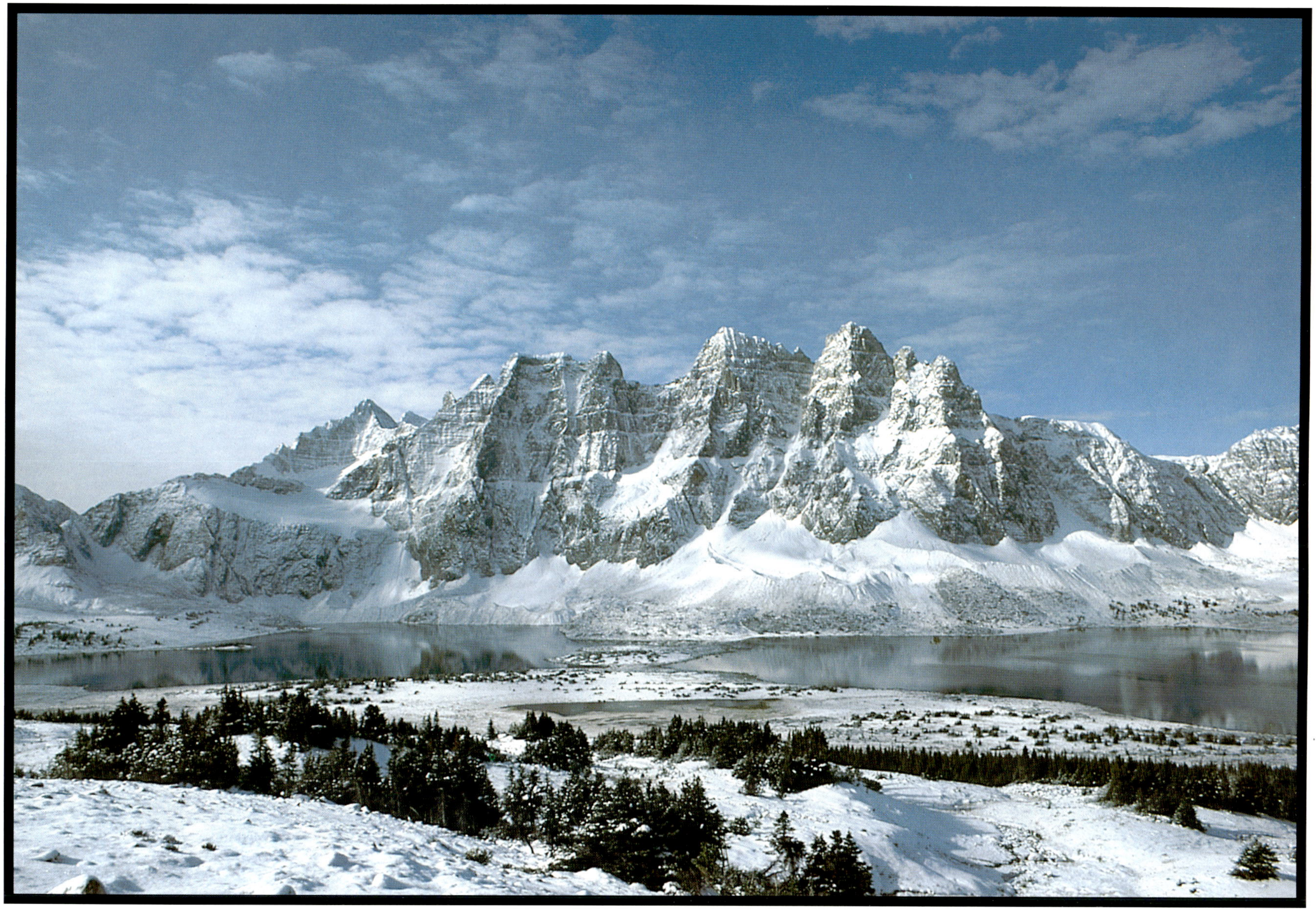

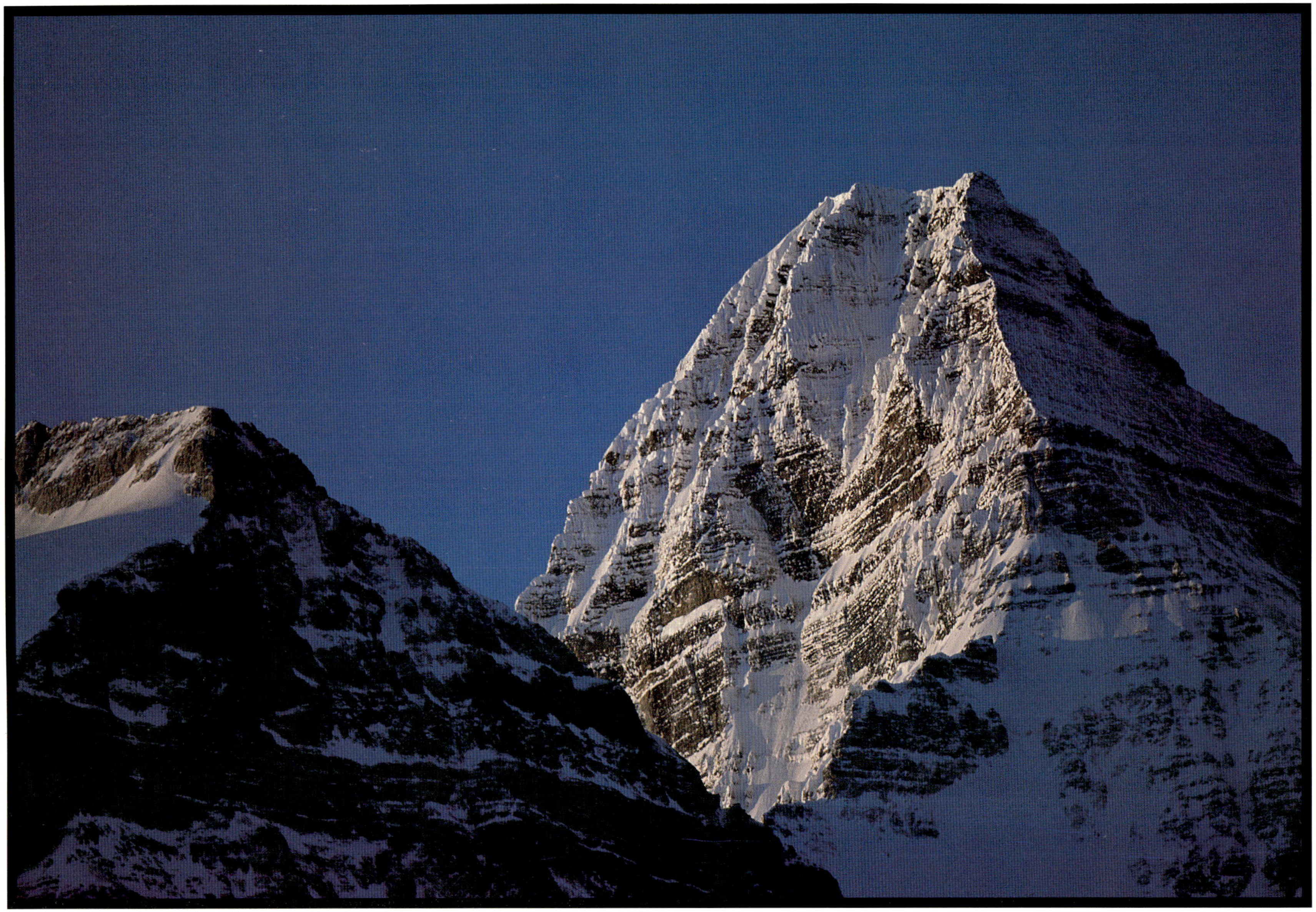

IMAGE #19 MOUNT ASSINABOINE

IMAGE #20 SUNRISE FROM MOUNT BRYCE

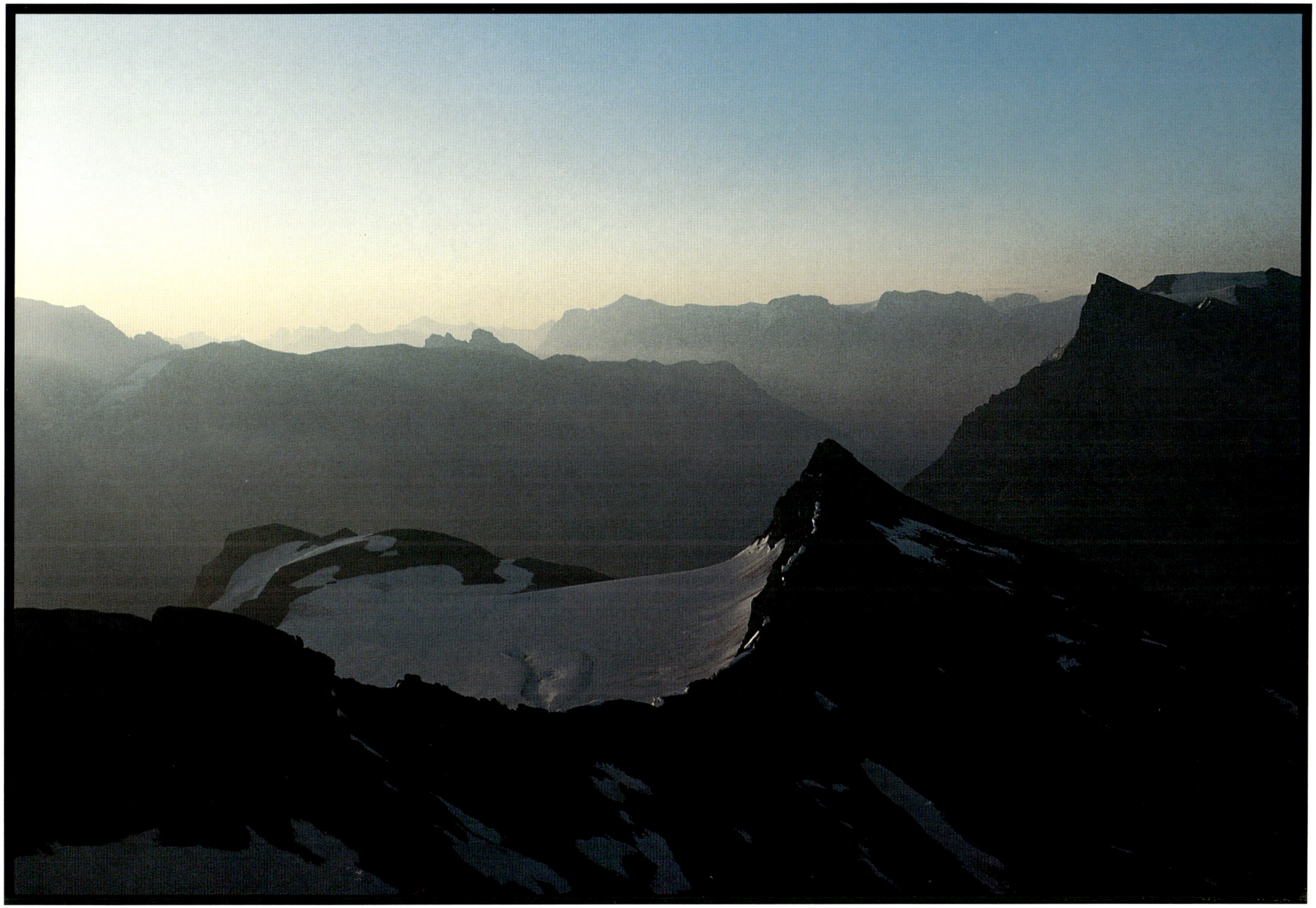

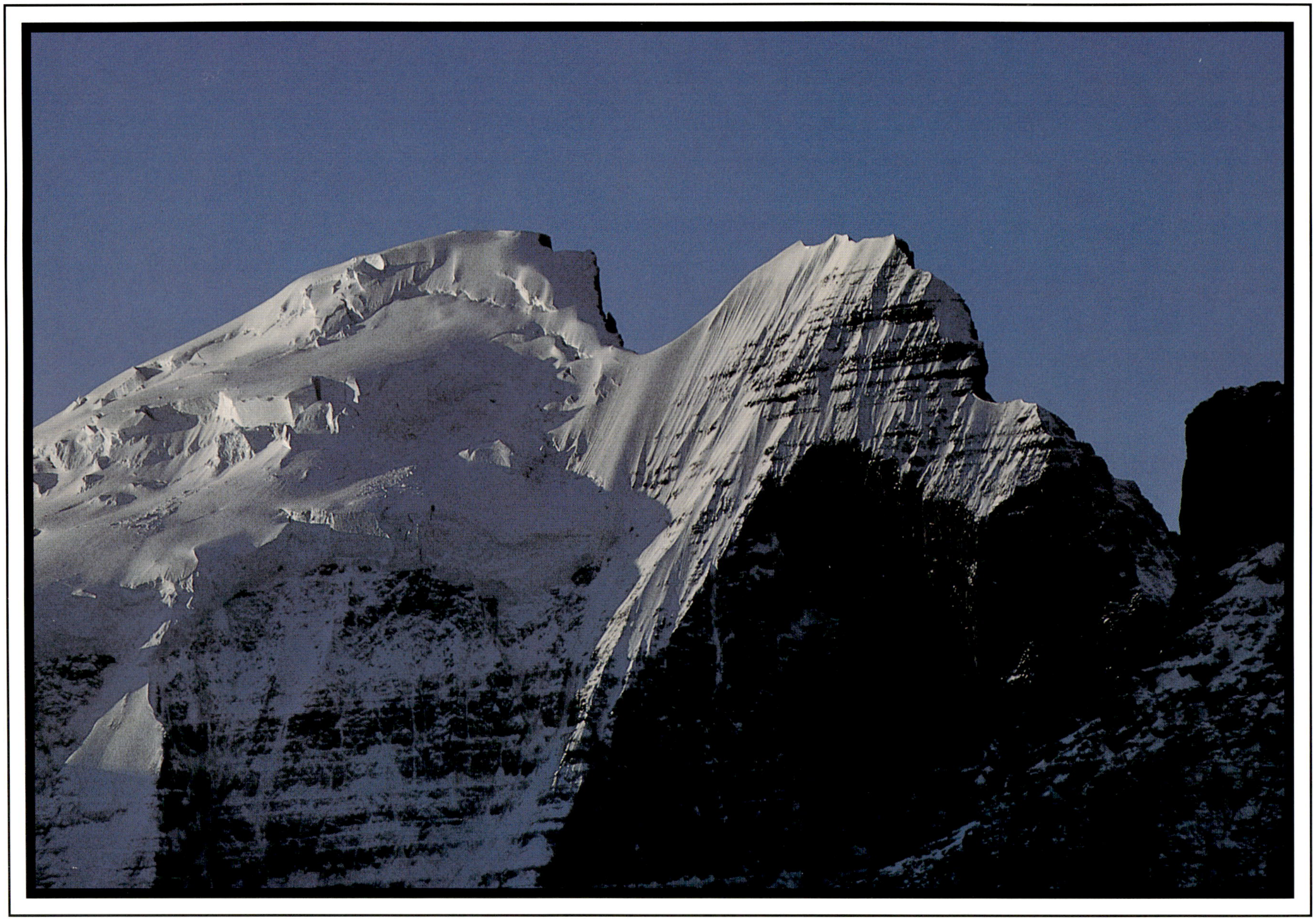

IMAGE #21 NORTH TWIN, NORTH FACE

IMAGE #22 THE TWINS

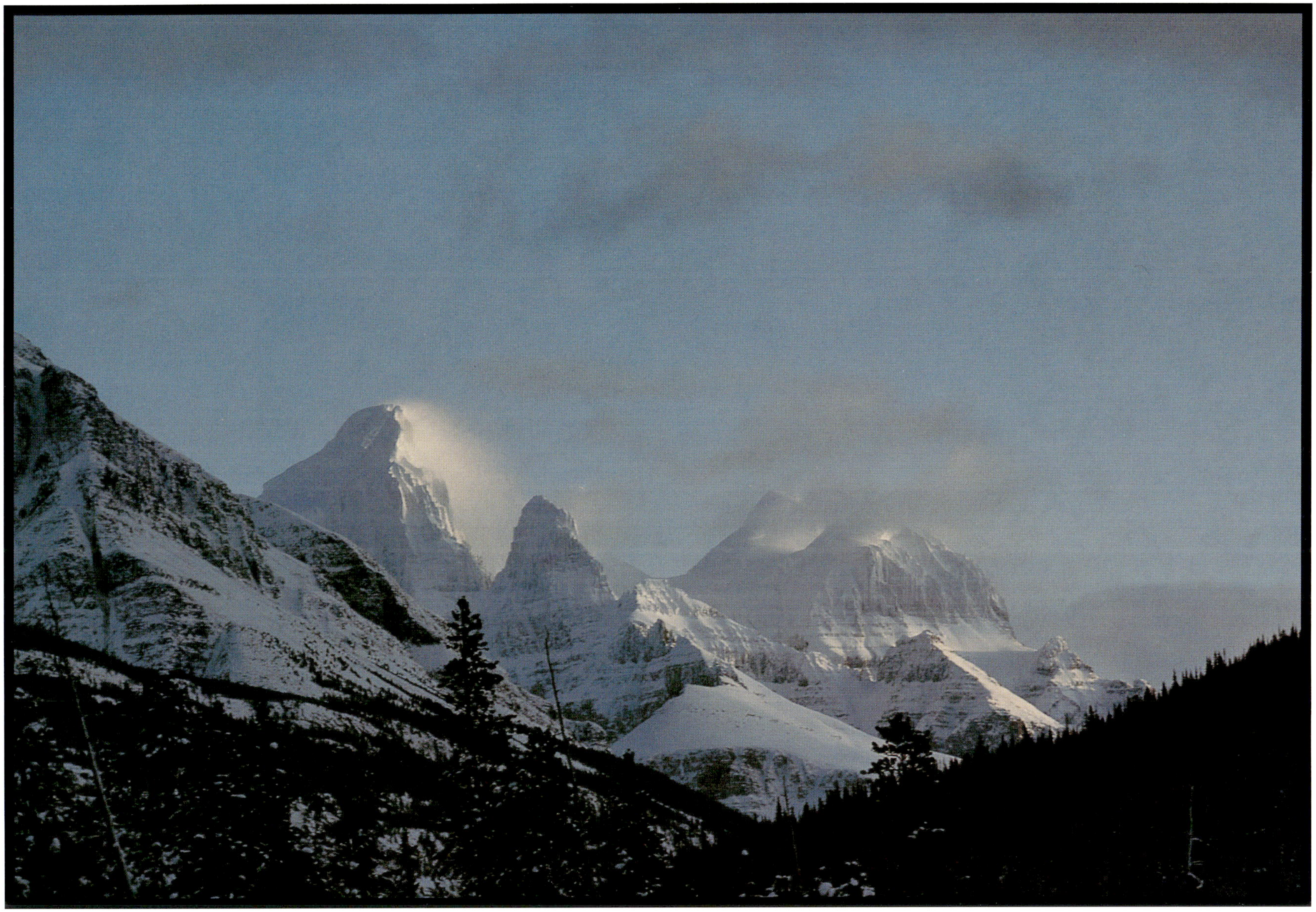

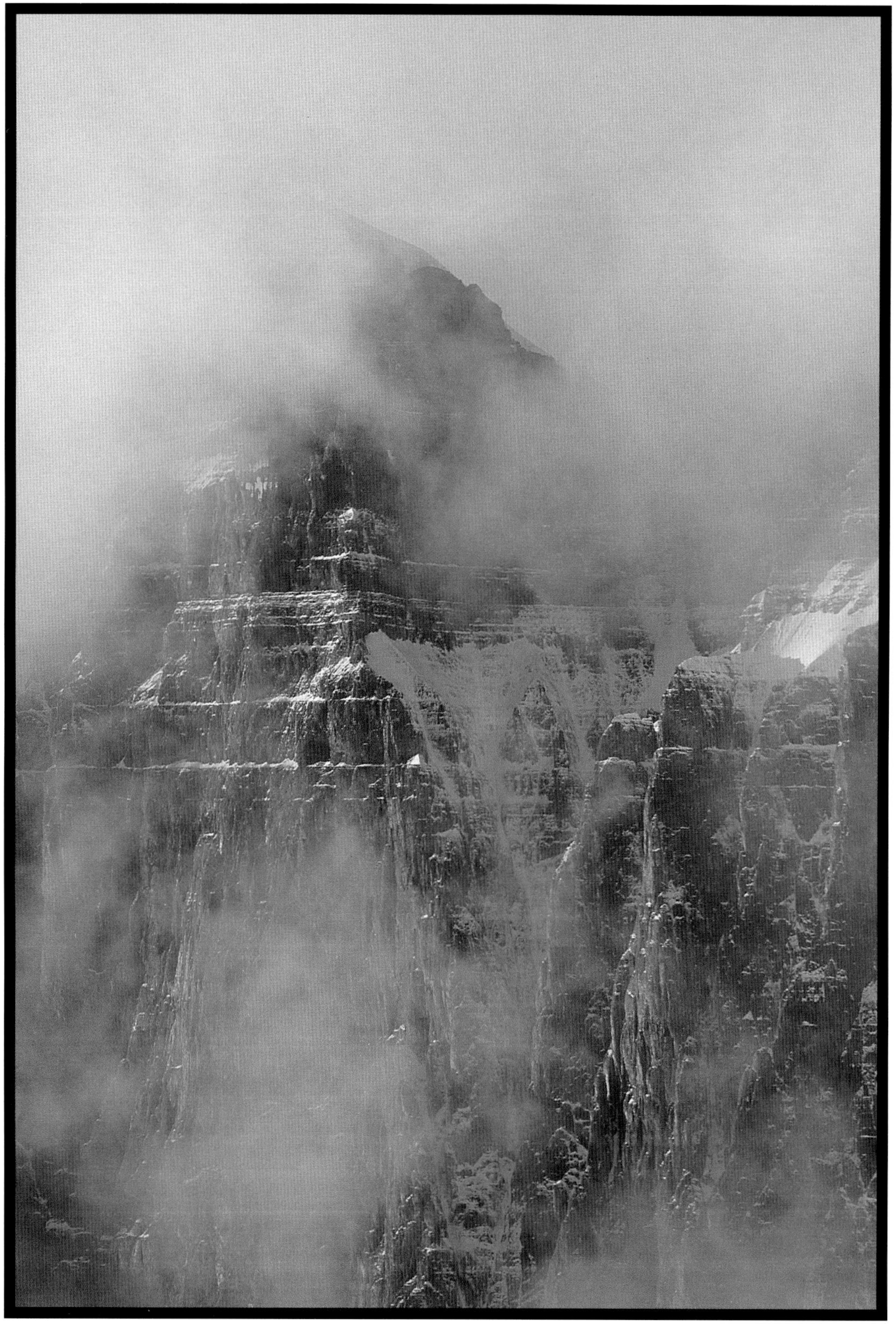

IMAGE #23 NORTH TWIN, WEST FACE

IMAGE #24   TWINS TOWER

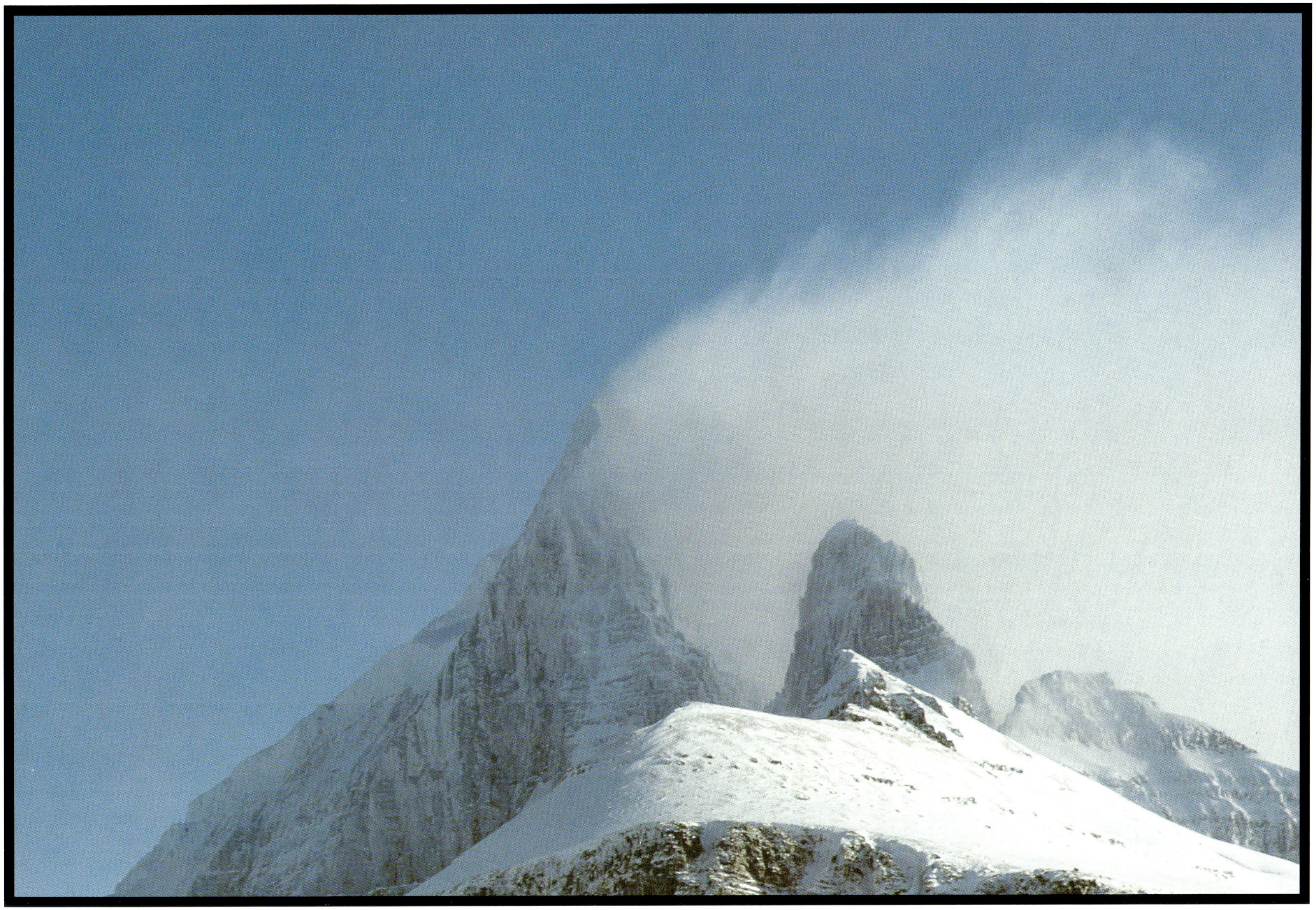

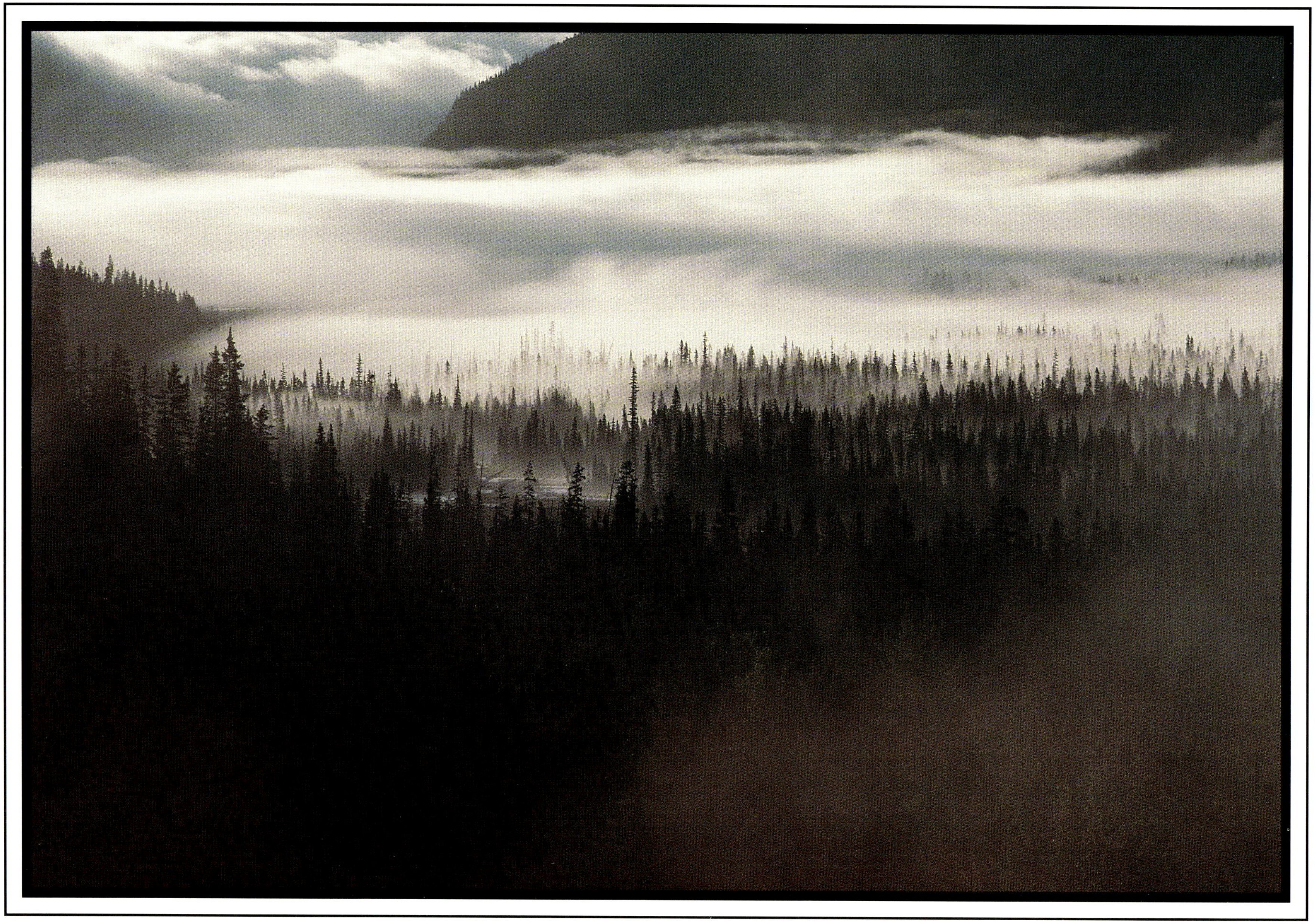

IMAGE #25 GLACIER RIVER VALLEY

IMAGE #26 MOUNT WOOLLEY

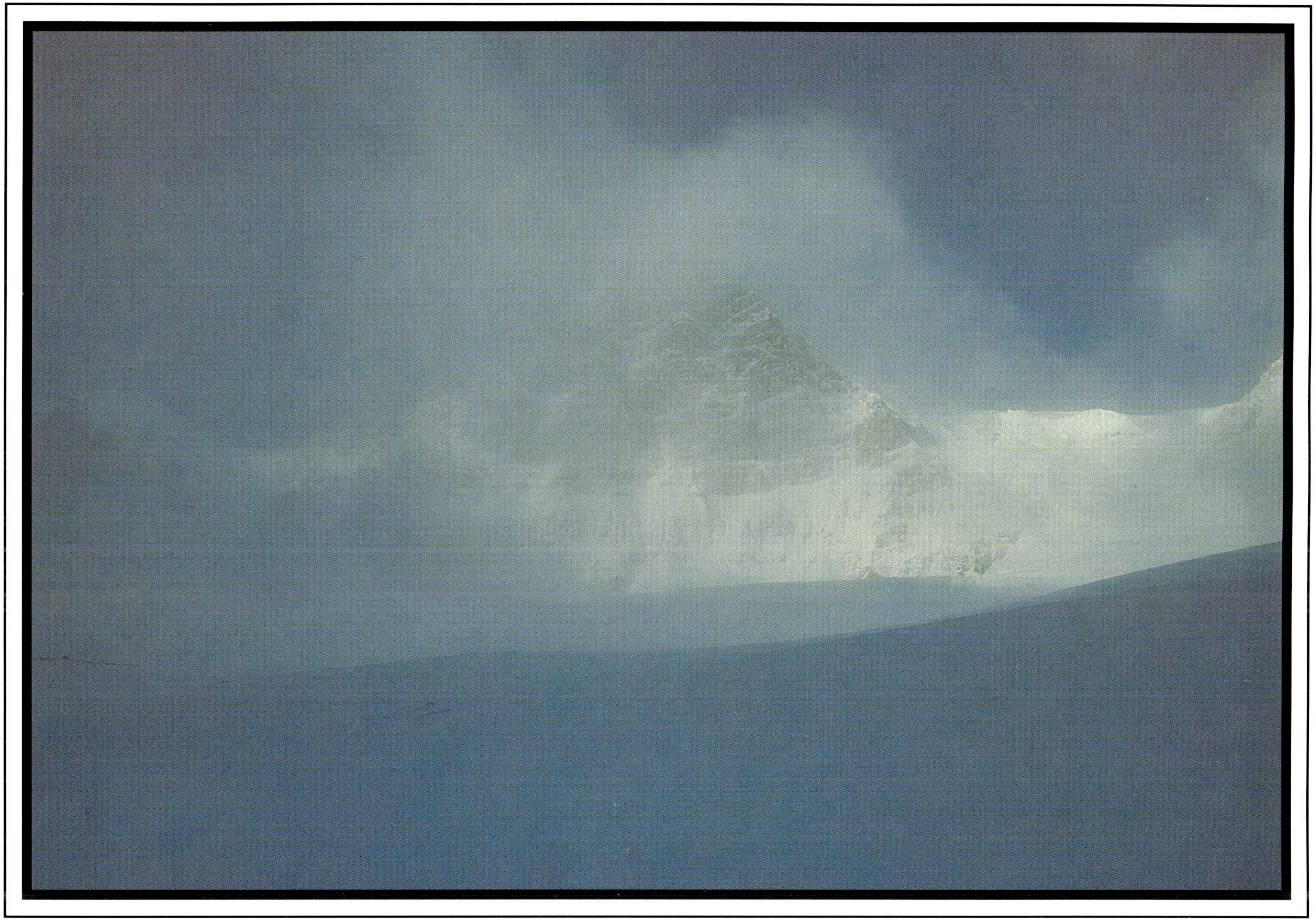

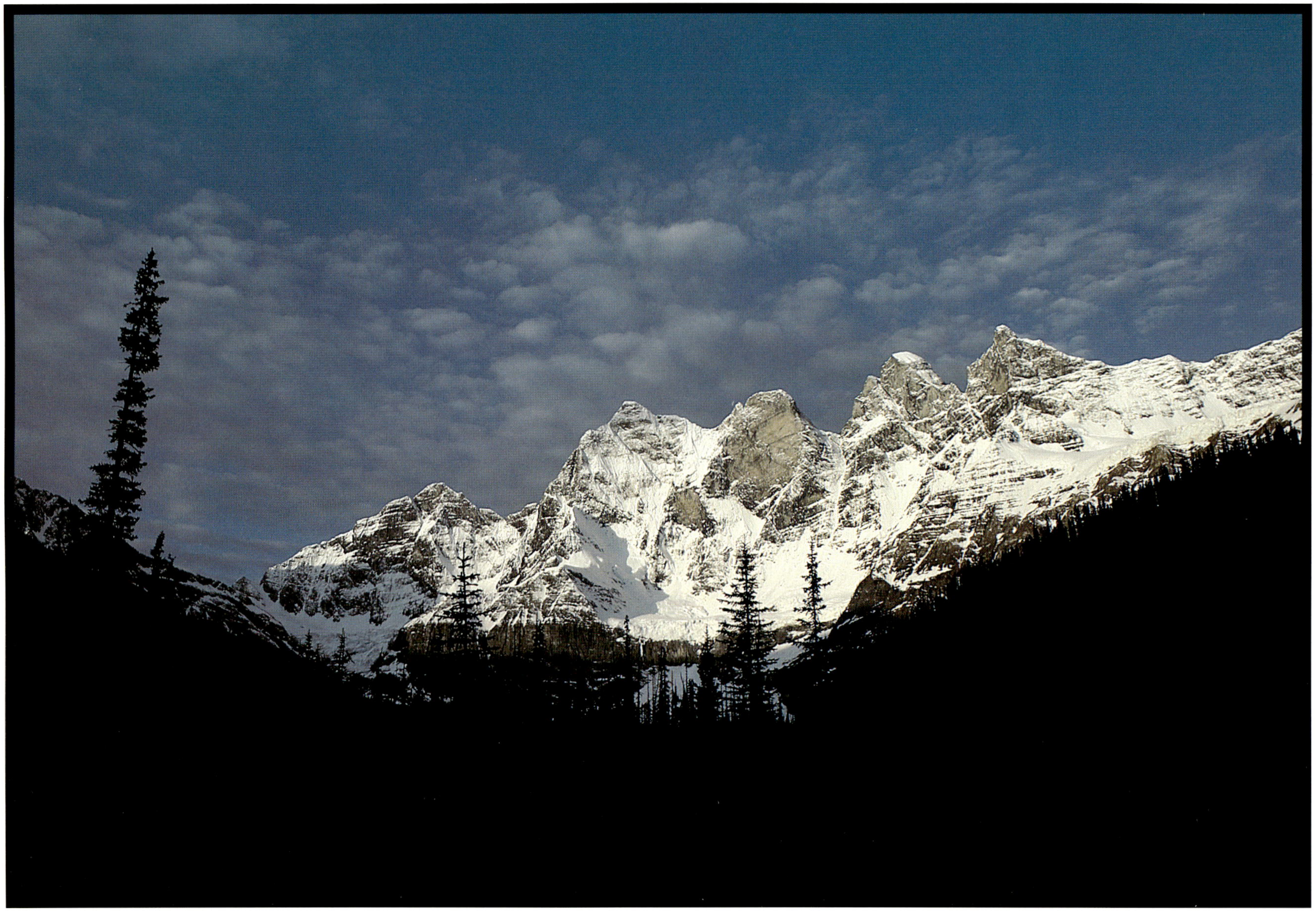

IMAGE #27 THE GOODSIR TOWERS

IMAGE #28 THE SOUTH GOODSIR TOWER

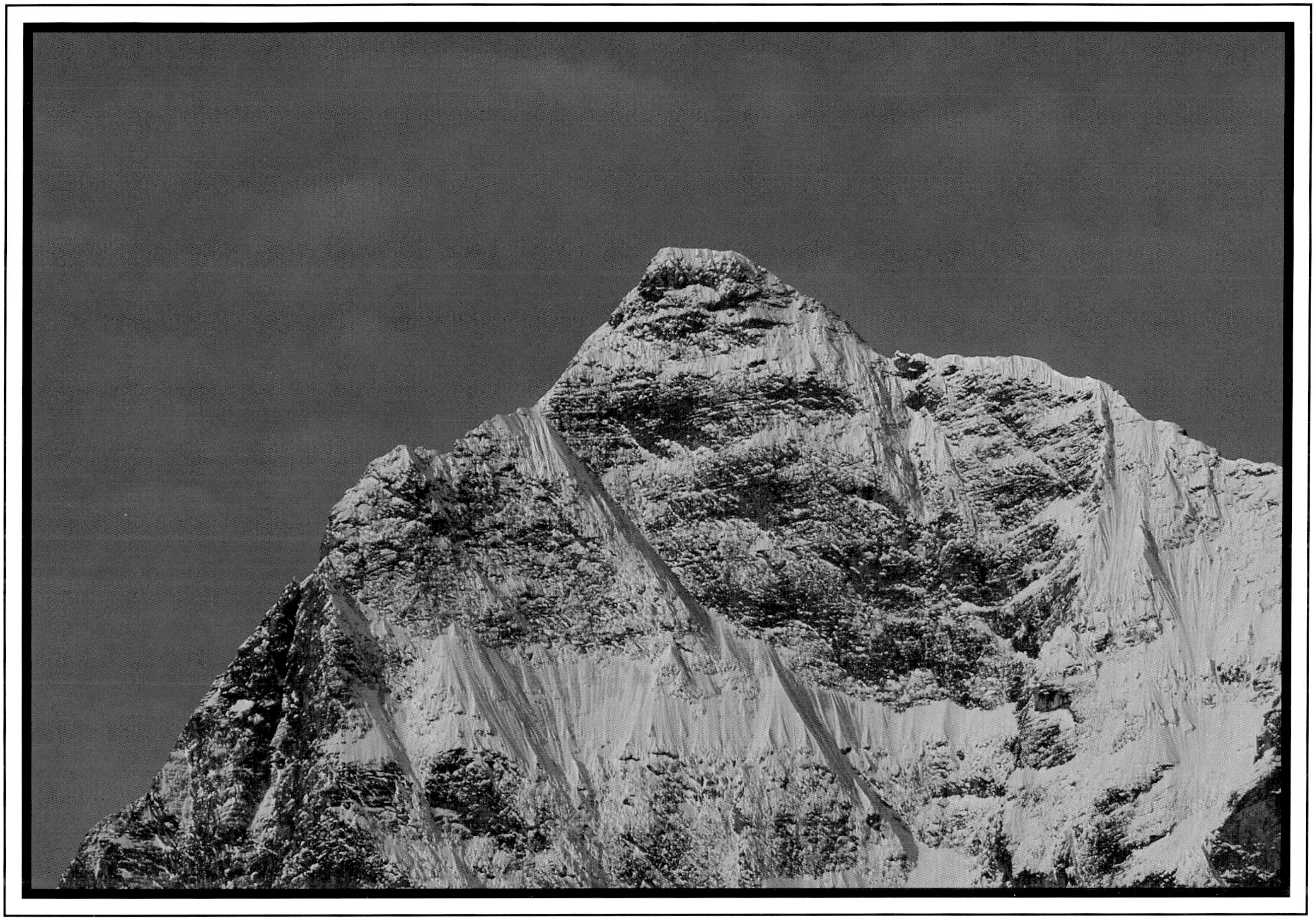

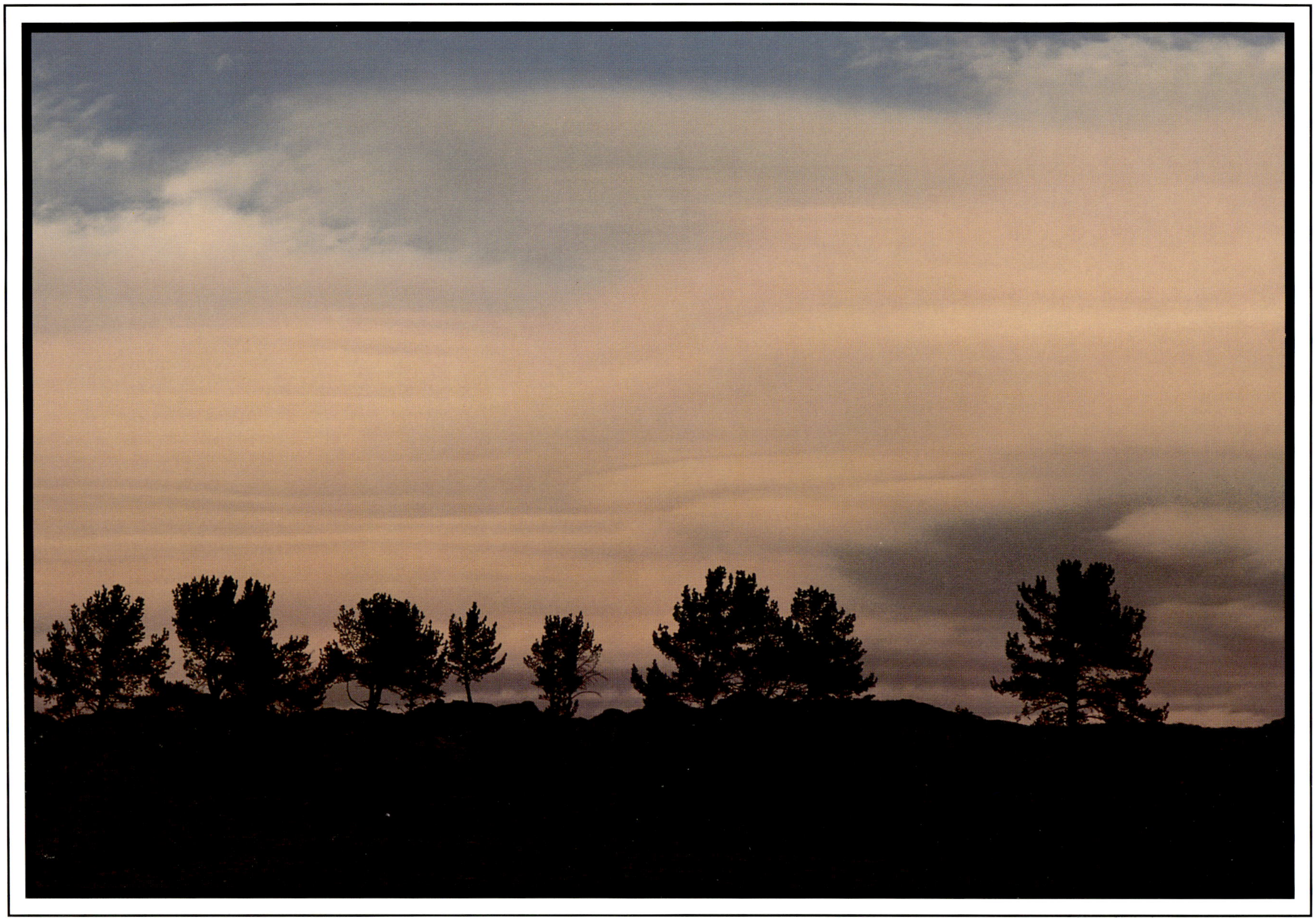

IMAGE #29 CHINOOK CLOUDS

IMAGE #30 SNOW DOME

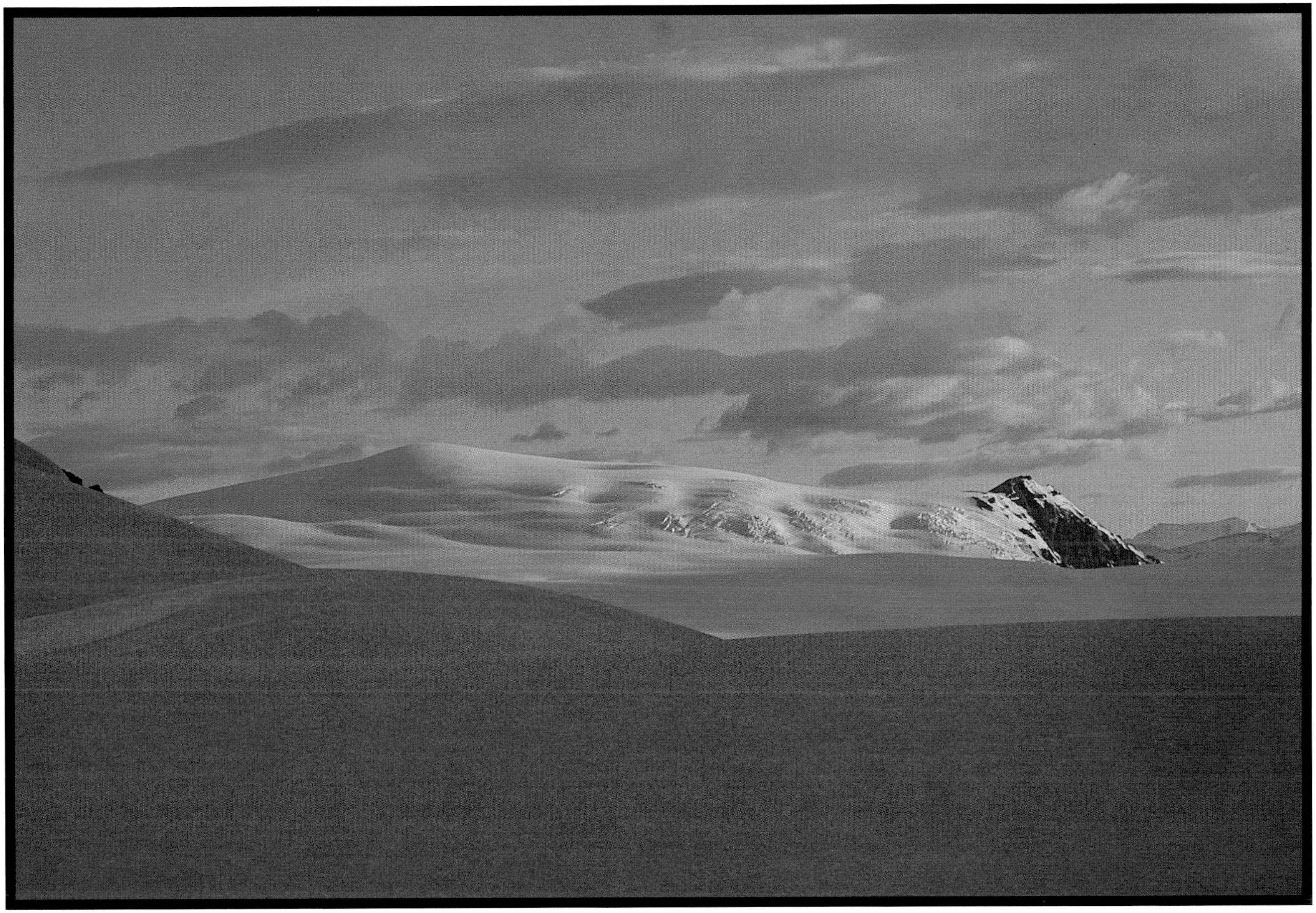

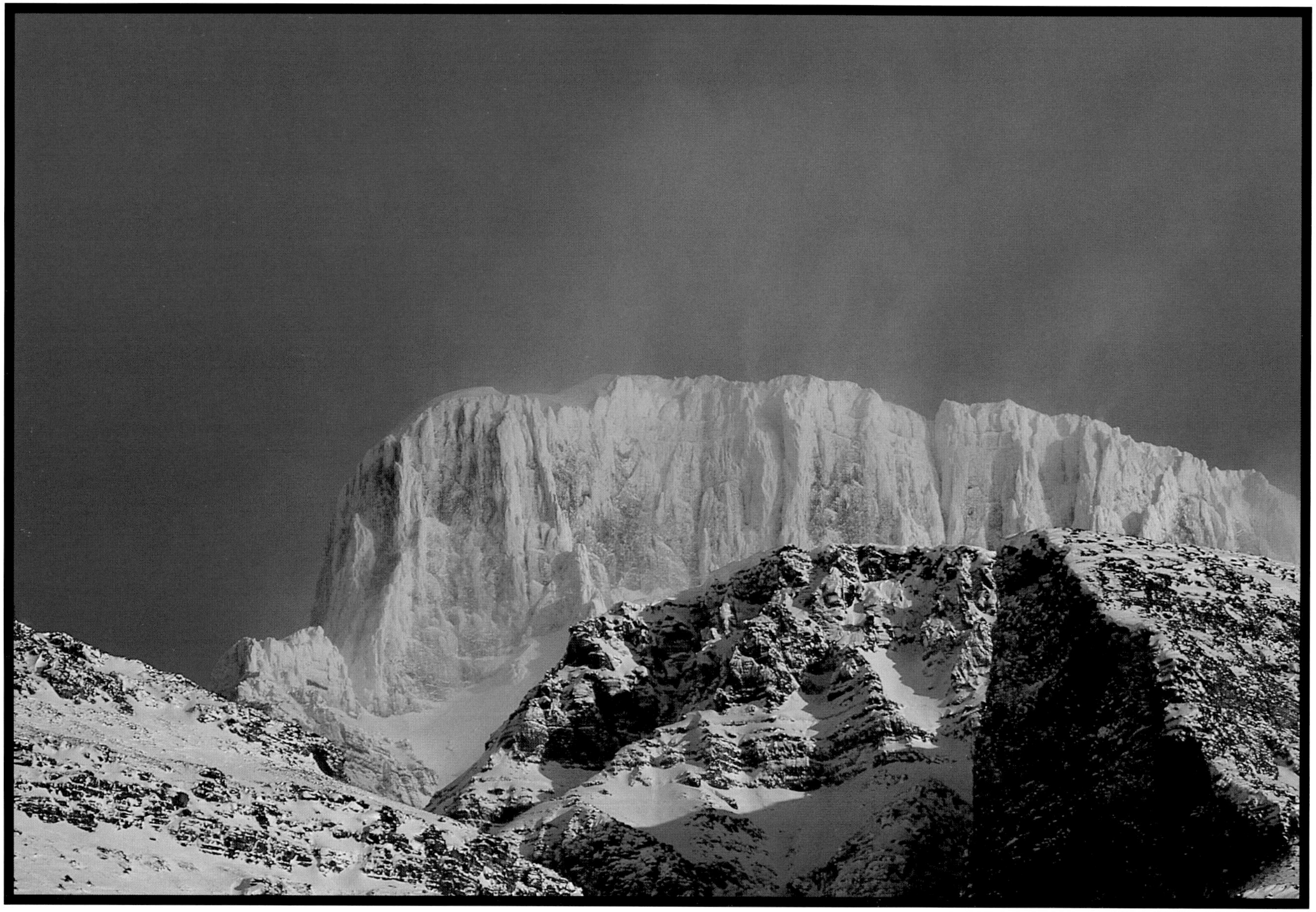

IMAGE #31 MOUNT ALBERTA

IMAGE #32 MOUNT ALBERTA, MOONRISE

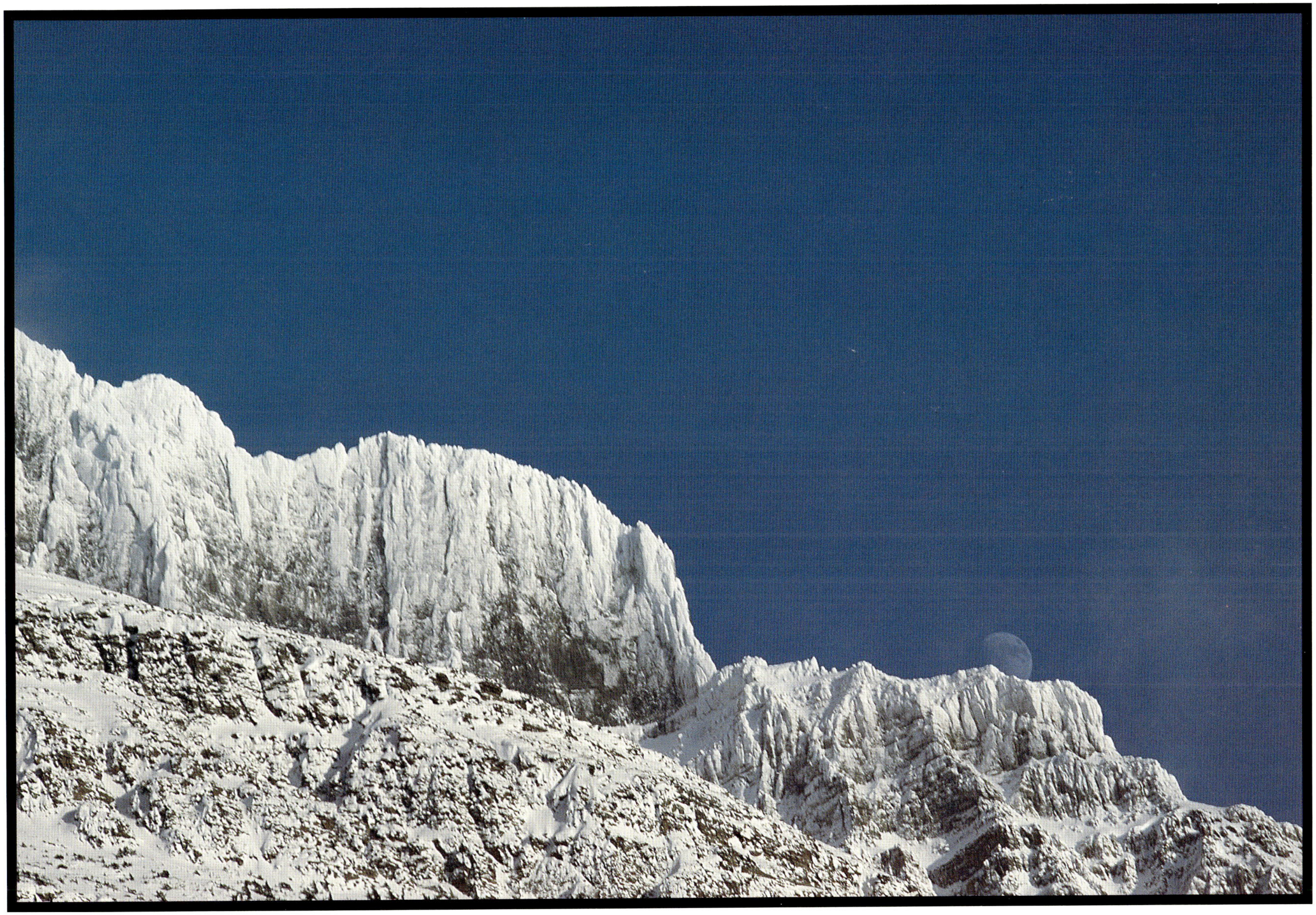

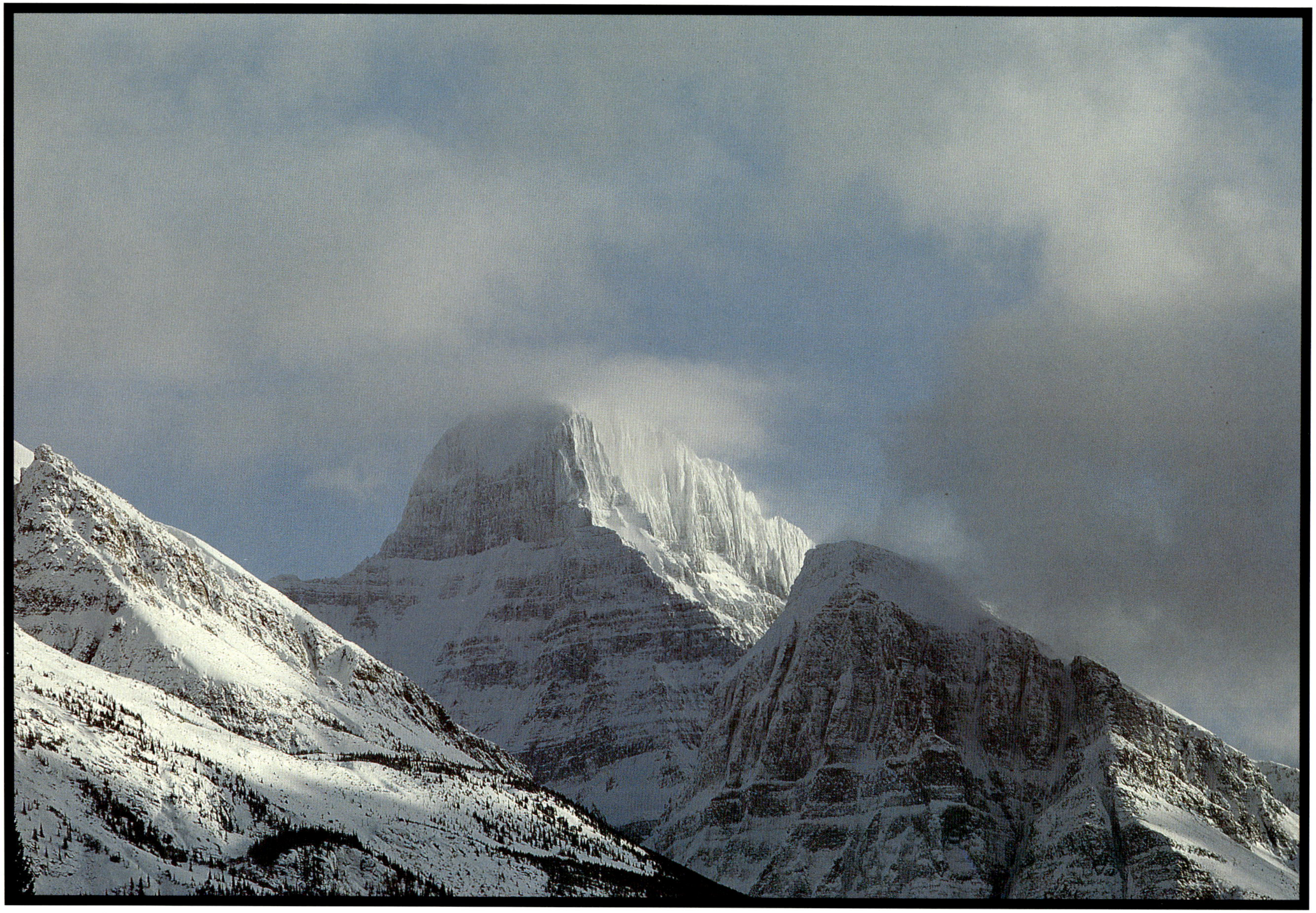

IMAGE #33 MOUNT ALBERTA

IMAGE #34 NIGEL CREEK

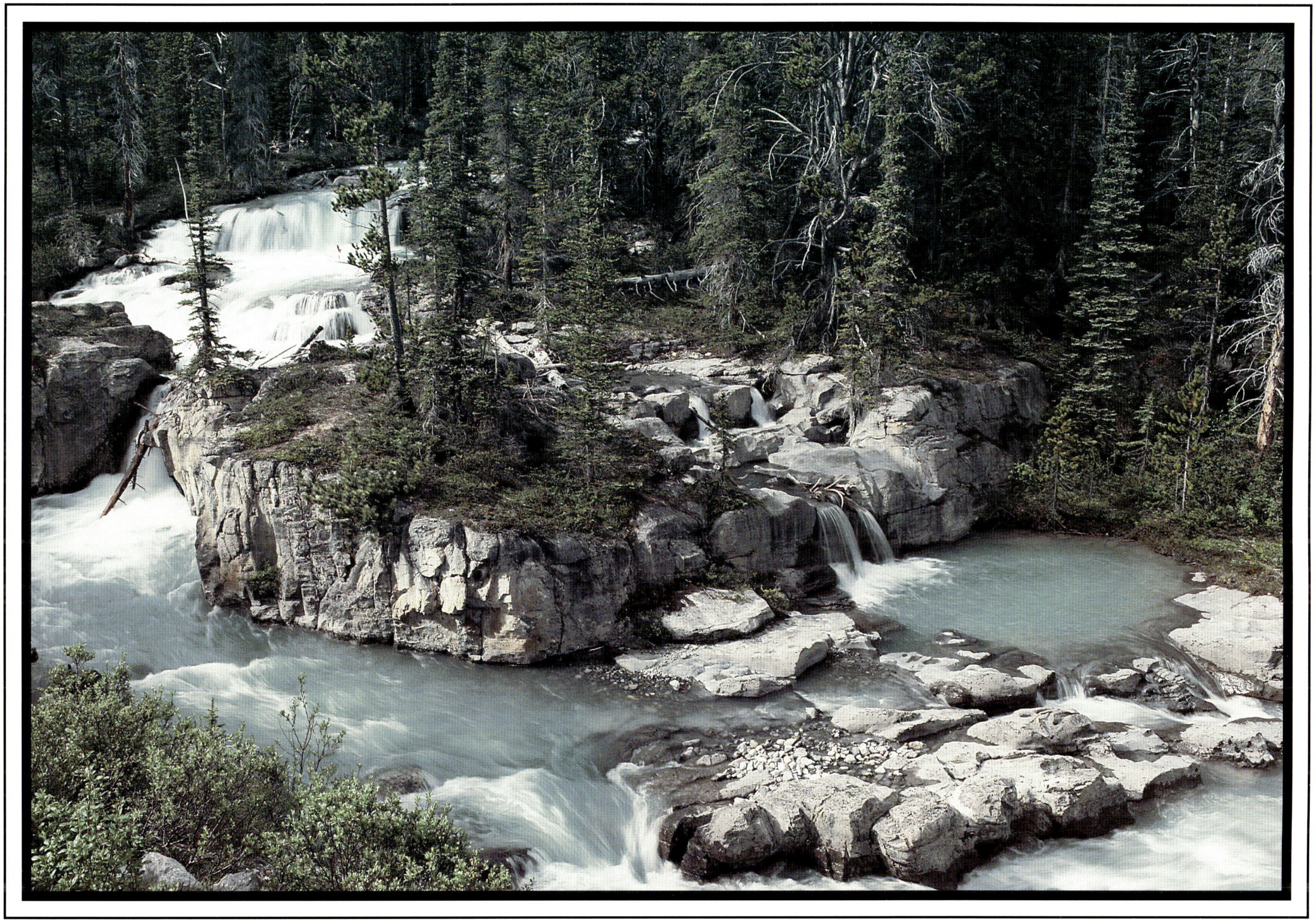

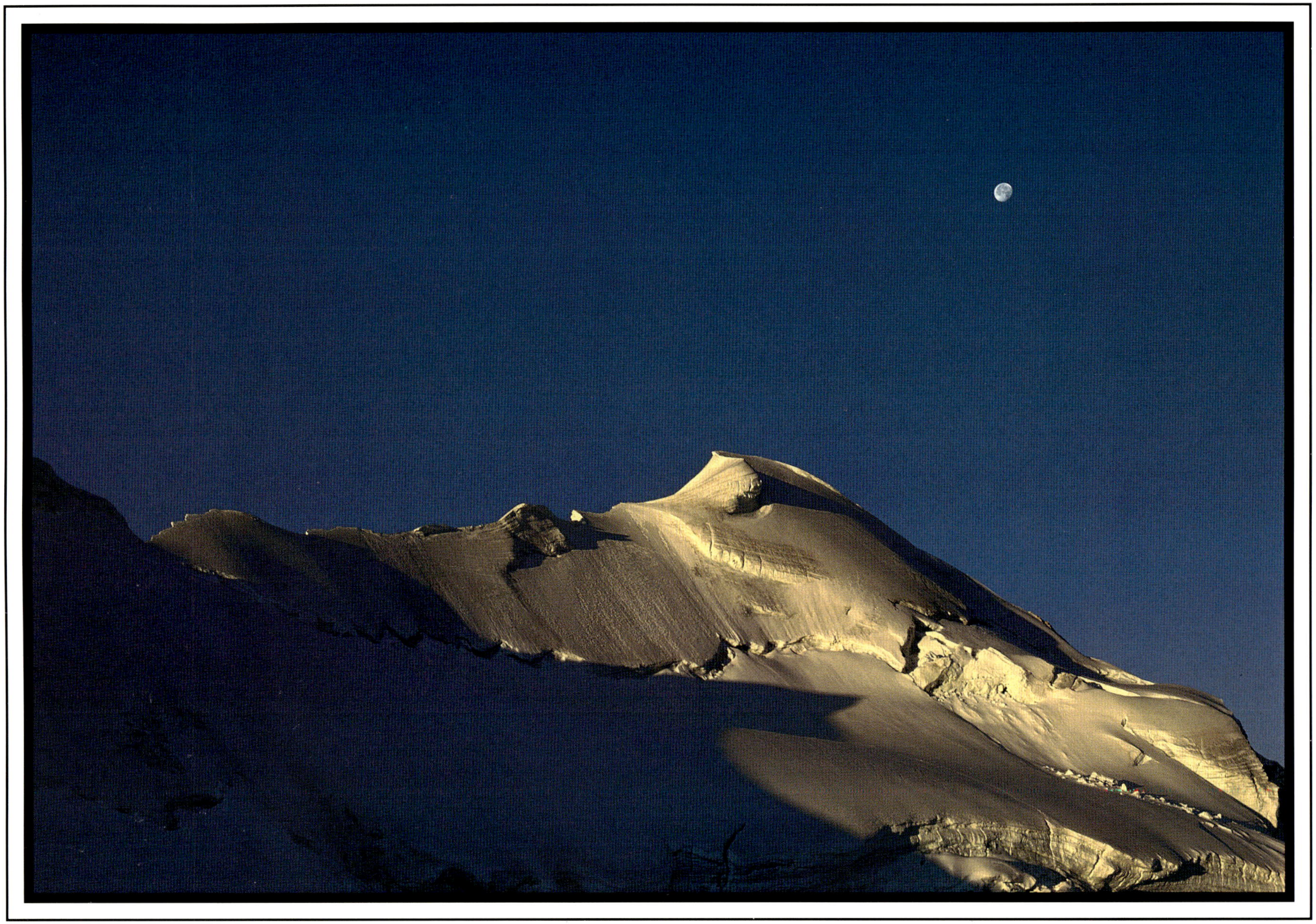

IMAGE #35 MOUNT TEMPLE, SUNRISE

IMAGE #36 MOUNT KITCHENER

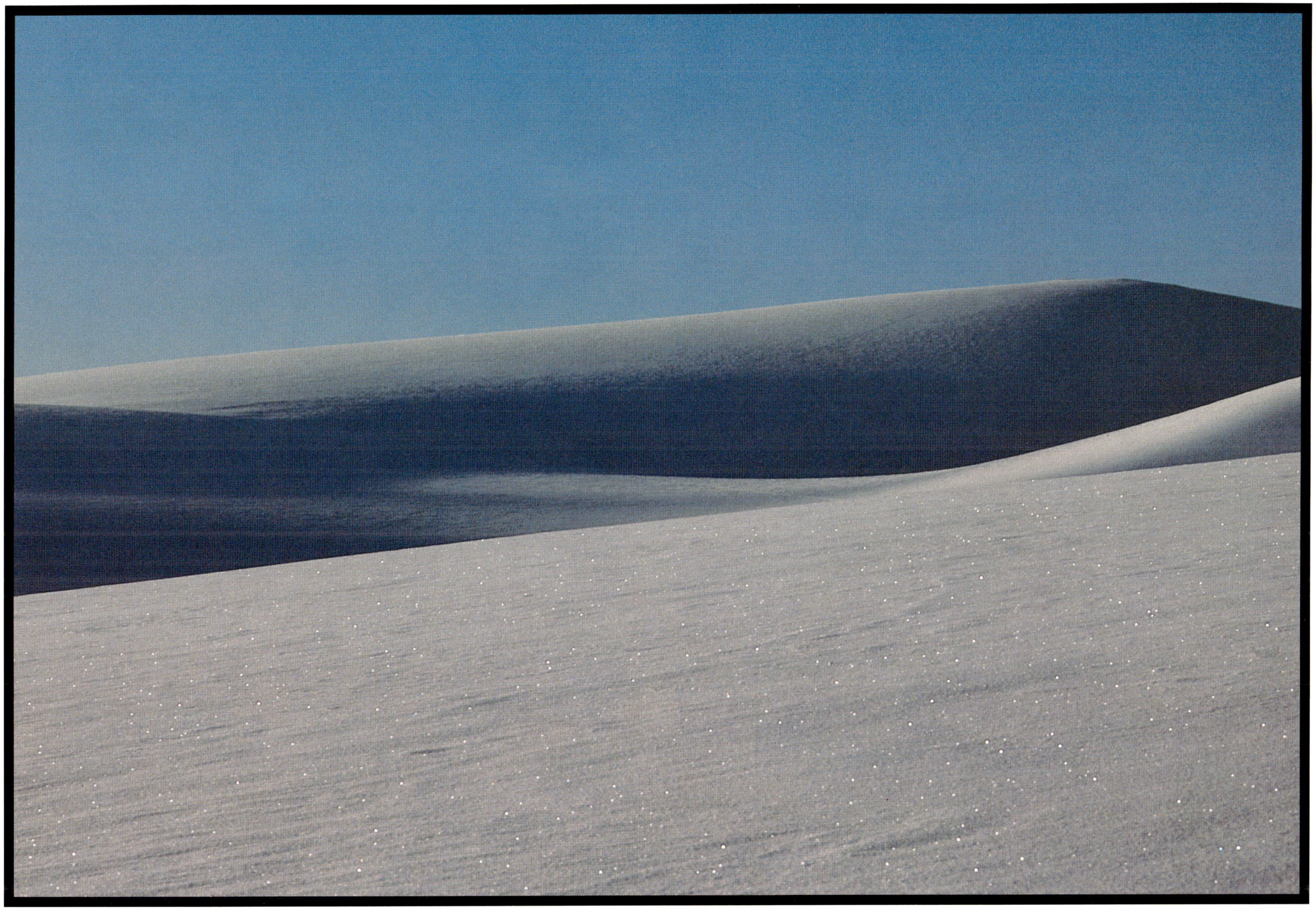

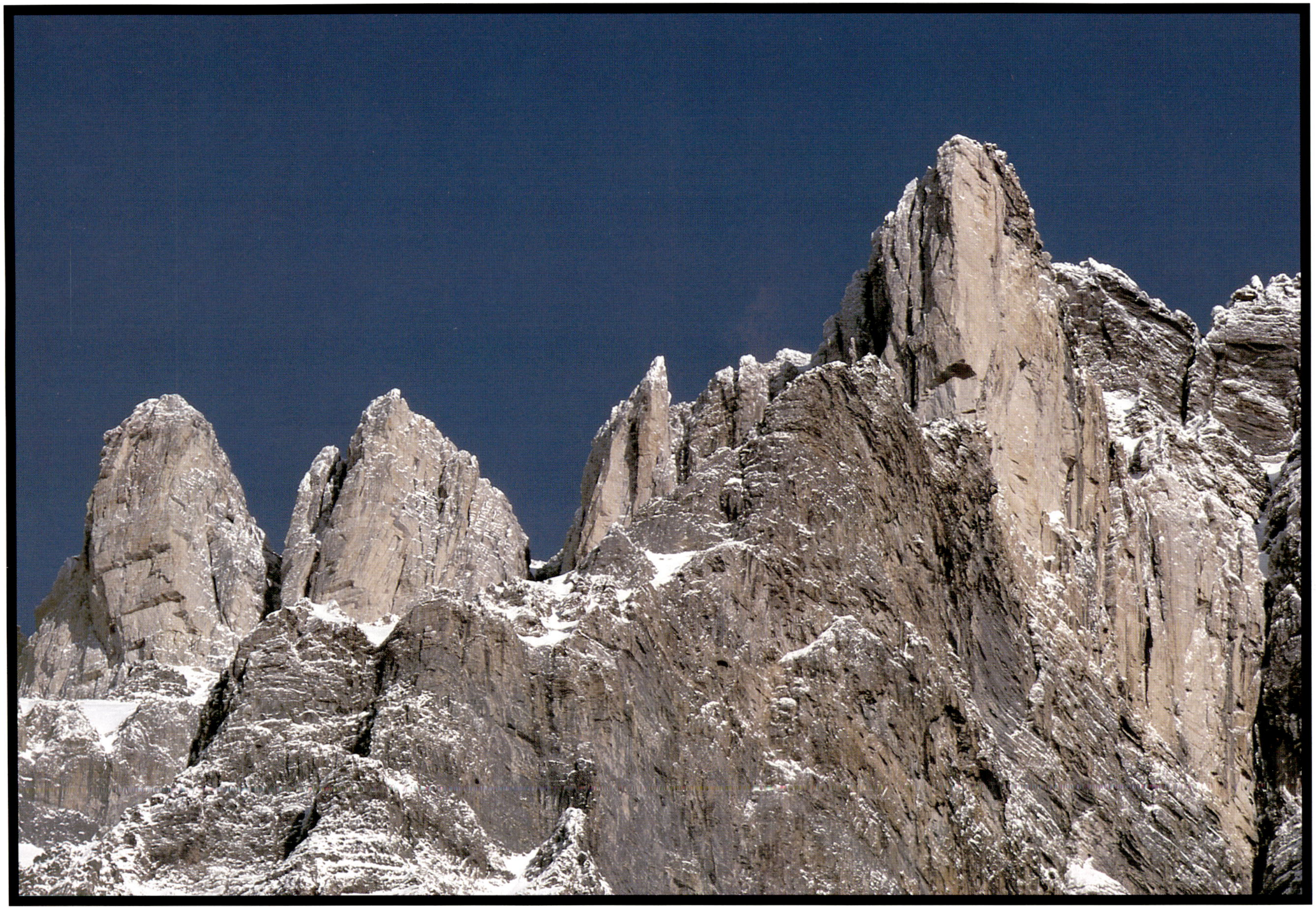

IMAGE #37 MOUNT WILSON TOWERS

IMAGE #38 TOWERS AND CLOUDS

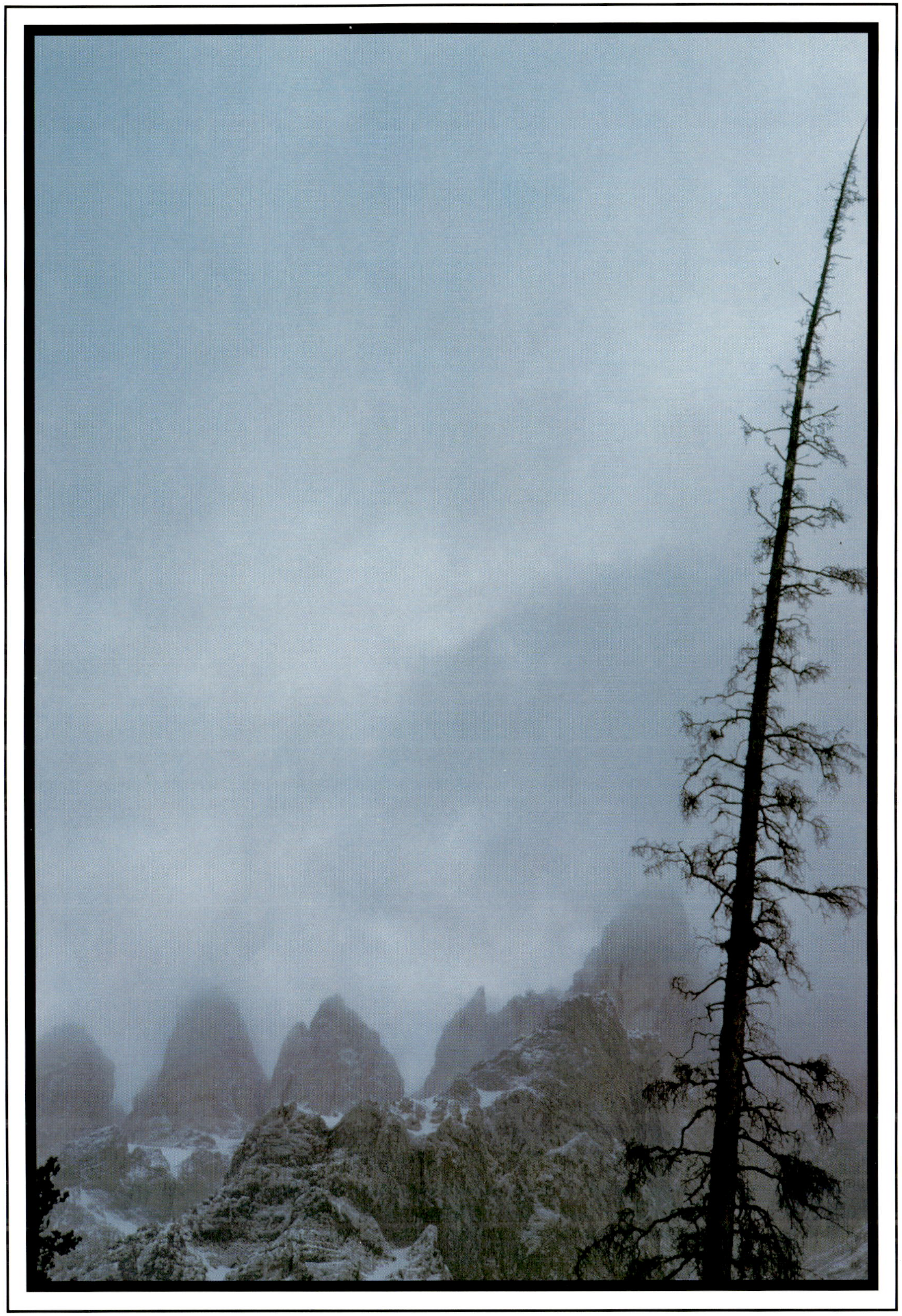

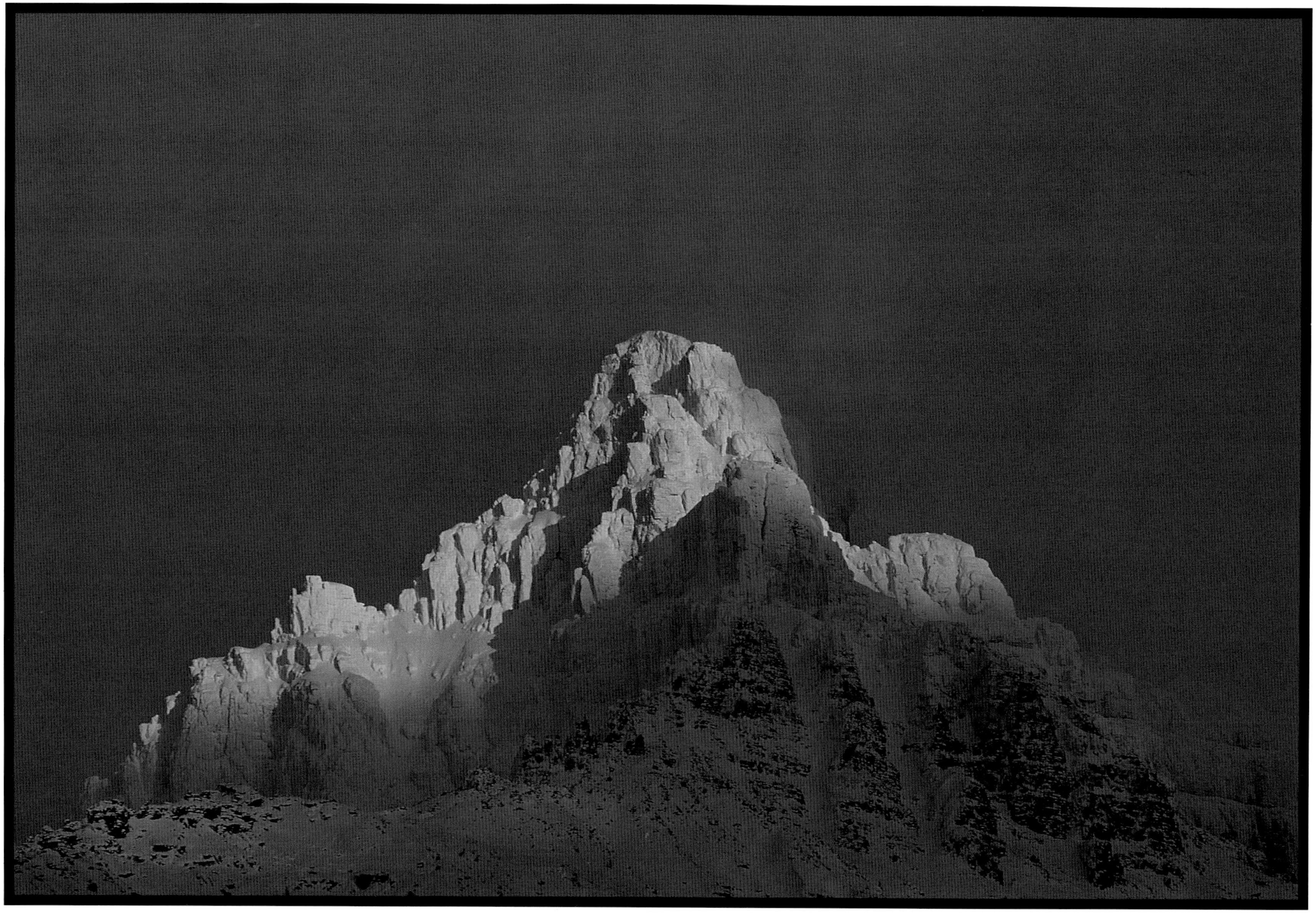

IMAGE #39 MOUNT CONFEDERATION

IMAGE #40 ATHABASCA RIVER VALLEY

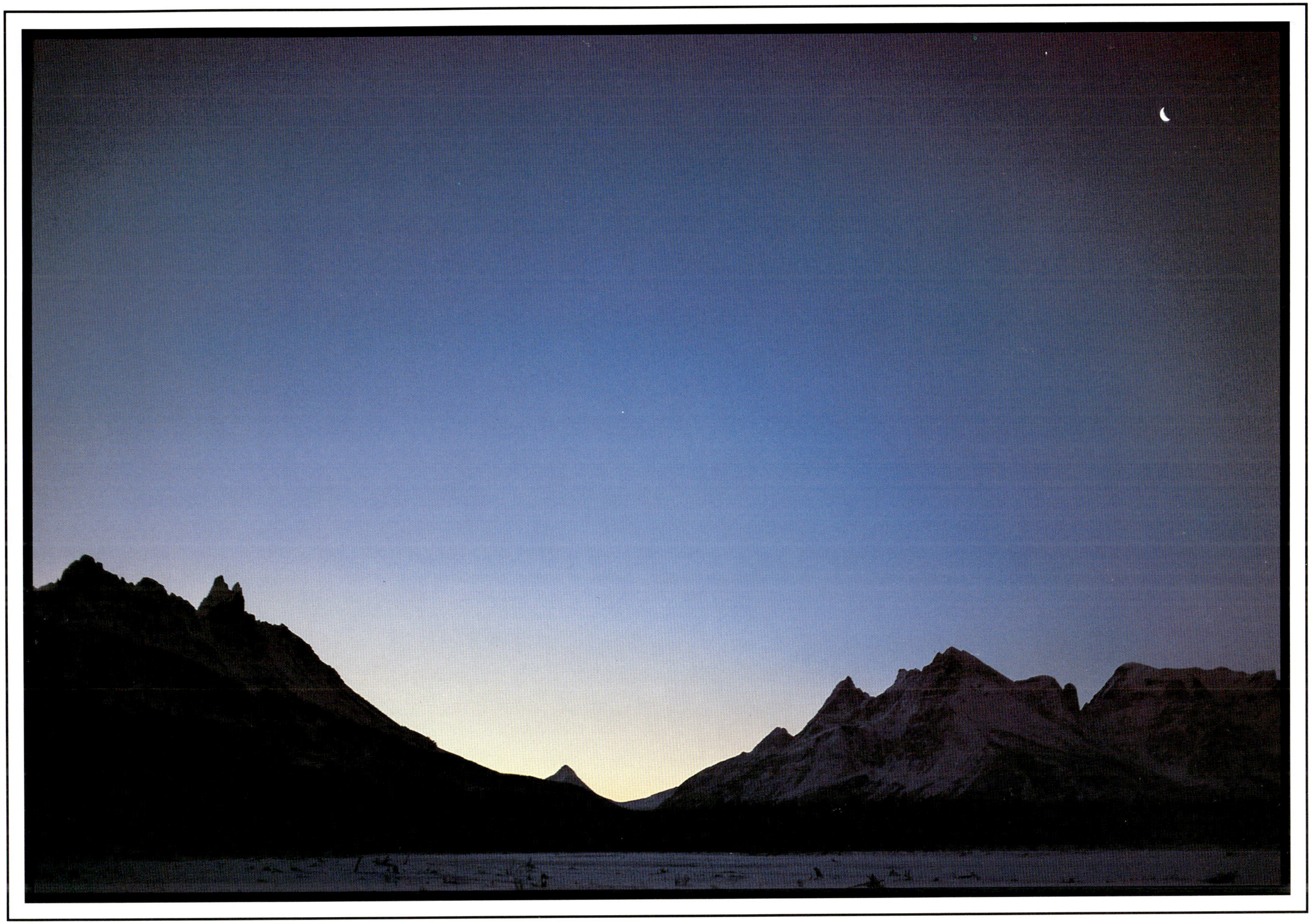

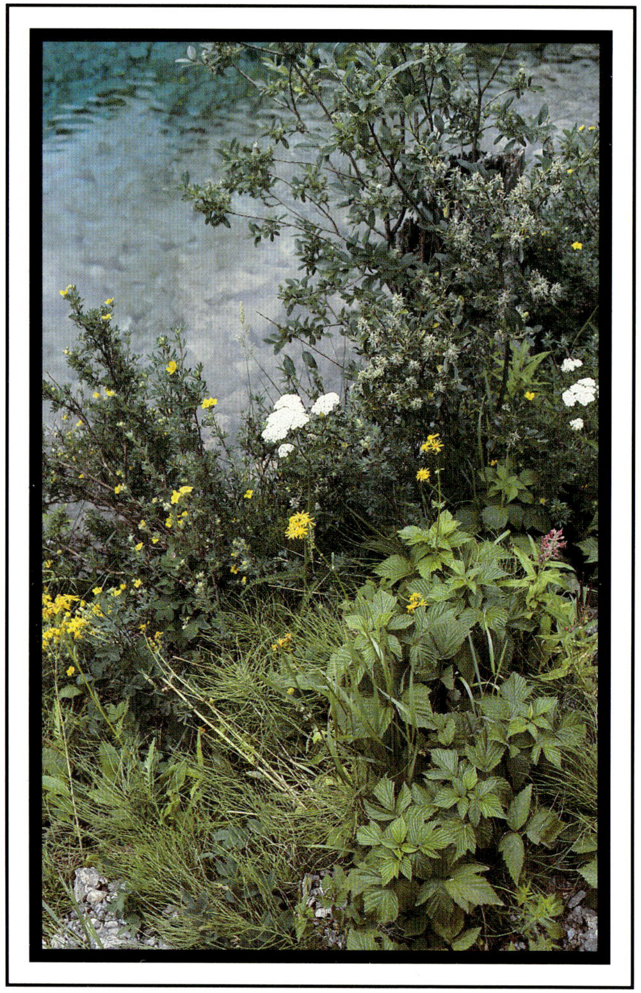

NOTES ON THE PHOTOGRAPHS

IMAGE #1 MOUNT FORBES, 1988
Looking across from the Lyell Icefield, this view is of the Northwest face.

IMAGE #2 MOUNT BRYCE, 1989
Taken from the Columbia Icefield in winter, this image shows the North face in the evening sun.

IMAGE #3 LAKE OESA, 1979
Looking across from Wiwaxy Peak, Lake Oesa is the highest lake.

IMAGE #4 GERALDINE LAKE, 1988
The first Geraldine Lake after a fall storm.

IMAGE #5 MOUNT ATHABASCA, 1987
Taken from the Icefields Parkway in winter, this perspective shows the East face at sunrise.

IMAGE #6 GLACIER LAKE, 1984
Looking West from the East end of Glacier Lake, the Southeast Lyell Glacier is just visible to the right.

IMAGE #7 MOUNT FAY, MOONRISE, 1986
Looking South from Sentinel Pass, this image shows the North face in late fall.

IMAGE #8 MOUNT ROBSON, 1981
Taken from Resplendent Mountain. The righthand skyline is the "Fuhrer Ridge".

IMAGE #9 MOUNT ROBSON, SUNSET, 1981
Taken from Robson Pass.

IMAGE #10 MOUNT ROBSON, MOONRISE, 1981
Taken from the same location as image #9. The North face is almost directly below the moon, the "Fuhrer Ridge" is now on the left.

IMAGE #11 MOUNT ROBSON, 1989
This view is from Berg Lake.

IMAGE #12 SUNSET AND STORM, date unknown
Taken from Highway 1A looking West from the Castle Mountain area.

IMAGE #13 MOUNT COLUMBIA, 1981
The Southeastern perspective of Mount Columbia as seen from the Columbia Icefield.

IMAGE #14 MOUNT COLUMBIA, NORTH FACE, 1986
This view is from the small lake at the toe of the Columbia Glacier.

IMAGE #15 MOUNT COLUMBIA, MOONRISE, 1986
Looking out from the col between the South Twin and Peak 3360.

IMAGE #16 SUNSET FROM MOUNT ASSINABOINE, 1983
This is the view looking to the West from halfway down Mount Assinaboine.

IMAGE #17 THE RAMPARTS, MOONRISE, 1987
The view from the North end of Amethyst Lakes in winter.

IMAGE #18 AMETHYST LAKES, 1988
Amethyst Lakes and the Ramparts after a storm.

IMAGE #19 MOUNT ASSINABOINE, 1986
Taken from Magog Lake in winter. The Northeast ridge is the line between the sun and the shade.

IMAGE #20 SUNRISE FROM MOUNT BRYCE, 1985
Looking South from the East ridge of Mount Bryce.

IMAGE #21 NORTH TWIN, NORTH FACE, 1989
This is the top half of the North face at sunrise. Taken from close to Mount Woolley.

IMAGE #22 THE TWINS, 1984
The view up the Athabasca River Valley in winter.

IMAGE #23 NORTH TWIN, WEST FACE, 1986
Taken from the same location as image #15, this was the view in the opposite direction.

IMAGE #24 TWINS TOWER, 1984
Taken from the Athabasca River Valley in winter. The North ridge divides the clouds and the clear sky.

IMAGE #25 GLACIER RIVER VALLEY, 1987
Looking East from the trail to the Lyell Icefield. Glacier Lake is lost in the mist to the upper left.

IMAGE #26 MOUNT WOOLLEY, 1987
This is the East face of Mount Woolley in winter.

IMAGE #27 THE GOODSIR TOWERS, 1987
The view from Goodsir Creek in winter. The South Goodsir Tower is on the left.

IMAGE #28 THE SOUTH GOODSIR TOWER, 1987
A detail of the North face in winter.

IMAGE #29 CHINOOK CLOUDS, 1988
Taken in the foothills along Highway 1.

IMAGE #30 SNOW DOME, 1985
Looking North from the East ridge of Mount Bryce.

IMAGE #31 MOUNT ALBERTA, 1984
Looking up from the Athabasca River Valley, this perspective is of the West face.

IMAGE #32 MOUNT ALBERTA, MOONRISE, 1984
A detail of the moonrise over the South ridge.

IMAGE #33 MOUNT ALBERTA, 1984
Taken from the Athabasca River Valley. The North face is in the shade.

IMAGE #34 NIGEL CREEK, 1985
Taken from the top of the big bend on the Icefields Parkway.

IMAGE #35 MOUNT TEMPLE, SUNRISE, 1981
Taken from the East ridge of Mount Temple. This view shows the summit and the hanging glacier of the North face.

IMAGE #36 MOUNT KITCHENER, 1989
The setting sun on Mount Kitchener.

IMAGE #37 MOUNT WILSON TOWERS, 1984
Taken from the Icefields Parkway.

IMAGE #38 TOWERS AND CLOUDS, date unknown
A different perspective of the same subject as in image #37.

IMAGE #39 MOUNT CONFEDERATION, 1984
This perspective is of the West face after a winter storm.

IMAGE #40 ATHABASCA RIVER VALLEY, 1984
Taken just seconds before sunrise. Mount Columbia is in the center, Mount Quincy is on the right, Mount Confederation is on the left.

EPILOGUE

As I reflect on the ten years that it has taken me to complete this book, I feel satisfied that my task has finally been accomplished. However, as I look at the source of my inspiration I have become sadly disturbed about its future. For this reason I feel compelled to speak out on the subject of the preservation of the wildlands that we now call The Four Mountain Parks.* I do so not only out of gratitude for all that they have given to me, but out of concern for their future.

Even in the relatively short time that I have been exploring the mountain parks, I have noticed many changes. Not only changes in the physical landscape, but changes in the attitudes of many of the people who use these parks. I feel that people are becoming obsessed with a safe and sanitized wilderness, and go into the parks with the attitude that the mountains owe them an enjoyable and trouble free vacation. They seem to have lost touch with the realities of coping with a hostile environment and make demands upon the parks without consideration for the future of these lands.

If we are to preserve the integrity of our parks, I feel that it is important to look at what we demand from them and to consider whether this is in the best interest of the wilderness itself. It is my opinion that the parks should not exist as a playground or to amuse people; they should exist as our legacy to future generations regardless of present short term, political, or financial gains. Development and "progress" are processes that cannot be reversed. If we continue to demand more recreational facilities from our parks, eventually they will exist without substance. The beauty may still be there, but the wilderness will have vanished.

Our parks have given us a part of the world that we could preserve forever; a living museum on a planet rapidly running out of wilderness. It would be a tragedy to destroy something so special under the guise of improvement, deluding ourselves that through changing the wilderness, we were making it better.

My photographs have become a touchstone for this whole philosophy. I could not imagine the mountains without the wilderness; that would not be a world that my eyes would wish to see. These photographs are not just records of beautiful moments in the history of our planet, they are records of a wilderness largely untouched by man. Hopefully they will serve as a reminder of what is still out there and not, to future generations, a remnant of what once was.

Anthony Neilson
1990

*Banff, Jasper, Kootenay, and Yoho National Parks.

ACKNOWLEDGEMENTS

I would like to take this opportunity to include my thanks to the following individuals who have given their support and shown patience to me and my endeavors over the years:

Mark Bohnet
Hans and Pat Brygger
Steven Phillips
Walter Weber
and my family

I would also like to express my gratitude to all those, past and present, who have sought to preserve our environment.